A~Z
OF
QUILTING

Contents

3

EDITOR
Sue Gardner

EDITORIAL TEAM
Marian Carpenter, Lizzie Kulinski

DESIGN AND LAYOUT
Lynton Grandison

PHOTOGRAPHY
Andrew Dunbar

PUBLISHER
Margie Bauer

PRINTED AND BOUND IN CHINA

A - Z of Quilting

This edition first published in 2005
by Quilters' Resource Inc.
PO Box 148850 Chicago, IL 60614
Phone: 773-278-5695

ISBN 1-889682-38-1

General Information

By the needle you shall draw the thread, and by that which is past,

see how that which is to come will be drawne on.

George Herbert, Jacula Prudentum

Notes for using this book

Measurements

Both metric and imperial measurements are given in all instances throughout the book. Do not, however, interchange them, as they are only equivalents and do not always translate into exactly the same length. If you begin a project using metric measurements, use metric measurements for the entire project and likewise with imperial measurements.

Photographs

The photographs are designed to provide information about quilting techniques and processes in association with the accompanying text.

To add clarity to the pictures, contrasting threads are often used and many of the photographs use samples that are either larger or smaller than what you would normally use when creating your own project. In these instances, follow the instructions in the text even when your eye tells you that the thread colour, stitch length or whatever it may be that is shown in the photo, varies from the written instructions.

Materials

Fabrics

Fabrics types

Pure cotton fabric is, by far, the most favoured fabric for quilting. It does not pill and holds a pressed crease or shape better than almost any other fabric. It is an easy to handle fabric for both hand and machine work.

There are, however, many other fabrics available that can be used to create beautiful quilts. Indeed, crazy patchwork has traditionally incorporated such fabrics as silks and velvets. Quilts made of woollen fabric have a place in history.

Fabrics that contain polyester can be used successfully. You will find that they do not hold a crease as readily as pure cotton fabric and pins and needles will be slightly harder to push through them.

Above all, work with the best quality fabric you can afford. Cheaper fabrics will often have less woven threads per centimetre (or inch) than a good quality fabric. This means that they are more likely to become distorted as you work with them and are apt to disintegrate fairly rapidly.

Ensure the fabrics you choose are of a similar weight to each other and have similar care requirements that are suitable for the intended purpose of your quilt.

Preparing fabric

Fabrics, particularly cottons, need to be prewashed before using them in your quilt. This enables you to check that the fabrics are colourfast and allow for any shrinkage.

Before washing, place each piece of fabric separately into hot water and leave for several minutes. If the water becomes discoloured, rinse the fabric and repeat the process. Continue soaking and rinsing until the water stays clear. If a fabric continues to lose colour, it is better to discard it and find an alternative. Repeat this procedure with all the fabric pieces you will be using in your quilt.

Place all the rinsed pieces of fabric together in your washing machine and wash on a gentle cycle. If you have several small pieces of fabric, such as fat quarters, baste them together into one long strip to prevent them from twisting and unravelling as they wash. Alternatively, wash these pieces by hand. Hang out the fabrics to dry or dry them on a medium heat in a tumble dryer. The fabric will be easier to press when it is almost dry, rather than completely dry.

Hint: the ideal fabric for quilting by hand should be woven with about 30 threads to the centimetre or 75 threads to the inch.

Batting

The type of batting that you choose can have a marked effect on the appearance of your quilt. Batting is produced from both natural and synthetic fibres and each type has its own special characteristics. Today there is a huge selection to choose from and even within the four types featured in the chart opposite, you

Type	General Characteristics				Cost
Cotton and cotton/polyester blends	Warmer and heavier than polyester batting with a similar loft	Suitable for both hand and machine quilting	Clings well to fabric		Reasonably priced
Wool and wool blends	Very warm and wears well	Very easy to stitch through	Tendency to beard	Springy and resilient	Expensive
Polyester	Does not breathe like natural fibres	Very easy to stitch through	More likely to slip if quilting by machine	Resilient	Cheapest
Silk	Gives warmth without weight	Can be a bit sticky to stitch through	Easy to hand quilt Beards through cotton but not through silk fabric	Drapes beautifully	Expensive

will find considerable variation in their characteristics. A wide range of methods is utilized to produce batting. Some battings are coated with resin (known as glazing) to help prevent bearding. Others have the outer surface slightly melted (known as thermobonding) to solve the same problem. Needlepunching is a method of mechanically tangling the fibres of the batting to keep them together.

Always check the manufacturer's instructions to find out if the batting needs to be washed before using and how close your lines of quilting will need to be, to adequately keep the batting in place.

Be generous when purchasing your batting. It cannot only shrink in the washing process but the very action of quilting can also cause the batting to 'shrink'.

Threads

Special quilting threads are available for quilting by hand. These threads are extra strong and thicker than normal machine sewing threads. Normal machine sewing thread is recommended for machine quilting, piecing by both hand and machine, and for appliqué. Special machine quilting threads are also available.

There is also an enormous range of both machine and hand embroidery threads that can be used when embellishing your quilt with either embroidery or appliqué.

For patchwork and piecing, always use a thread that blends with the fabrics you are stitching. Light browns and greys are useful thread colours to try when joining dark and light coloured fabrics together.

Tools
Cutting tools
Rotary cutters

Rotary cutters have revolutionized patchwork and piecing. They make it easier to achieve perfectly straight and accurately cut edges to your fabric shapes and also allow you to successfully cut several layers of fabric at the one time.

They must be used with care as their blades are very sharp. Always cut away from yourself and ensure the blade guard is in place when you

general information

7

are not using the cutter. Replace the blade as soon as it starts to become dull. Using your rotary cutter in conjunction with a self healing cutting mat will prolong the life of the blade. It also makes it easier to cut fabric as the surface of the mat tends to 'grip' the fabric as you cut.

Scissors

Three pairs of scissors are recommended. Have one medium to large pair of scissors especially for cutting template plastic and paper. These materials tend to dull the blades more quickly than fabric.

Have a second large pair of scissors for cutting fabric and keep them exclusively for this task. Use a small pair of scissors for snipping threads and clipping corners. Ensure the blades of your scissors are kept sharp right to the tips.

Rulers

Numerous specialty rulers are made especially for quilters. Many are made from clear acrylic. These enable you to clearly see that fabric and grid or templates are all aligned as they should be. They are also excellent to use with rotary cutters as well as fabric markers. If you are serious about quilting, you will find that you build a collection of different rulers that all have their own special uses.

A ruler that is approximately 15cm x 61cm (6" x 24") and allows you to cut long strips of fabric is essential. You will find that a ruler with 30°, 45°, 60° angles marked on it is invaluable as well.

Markers

Both cutting and stitching lines need to be marked onto the fabric. The most important thing to remember is that any marked lines must be temporary and they must be clear enough to aid you in your particular task.

Always read the manufacturer's instructions and test markers on a scrap of fabric before using them on your project.

See pages 87 - 89 for further information.

Templates & stencils

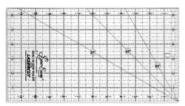

A plethora of ready made stencils and templates are available from specialist quilting shops, however you can use virtually any object you can comfortably trace around as a template.

Specialist quilting shops also stock firm, thin plastic suitable for making your own templates and stencils. Thin card or heavy paper can also be used, however do not use a paper that is too flimsy as it is difficult to use without distorting your design.

Graph paper and isometric paper are useful aids for creating accurate geometric shapes.

See pages 14 - 15 and 87 for further information.

Fasteners

Safety pins

Safety pins, approximately 25-35mm (1 - 1 ¹/₂") long, are excellent for pin basting. They allow you to hold the layers of your quilt firmly together without needing to get your hand beneath the quilt.

See page 91 for further information.

Glass headed pins

Always use glass headed pins rather than pins with plastic heads. This way you don't run the risk of inadvertently pressing a pin and having it melt onto your fabric. Pins with small glass heads are less likely to cause fabric distortion but are still easy to see in your fabric (or on the floor!).

Clips

Bulldog clips are helpful for holding lining fabric out flat when you are layering and basting your quilt together.

Tape

Masking tape is a useful alternative to the clips mentioned above. In fact you will find numerous occasions when it will come in handy. Do not use masking tape that is too old as, with time, the glue deteriorates and can mark your fabric.

Hoops and frames

Hoops

Quilting hoops are generally between 35cm and 45cm in diameter (14 - 18"). The length of your arm will determine the most appropriate size hoop to

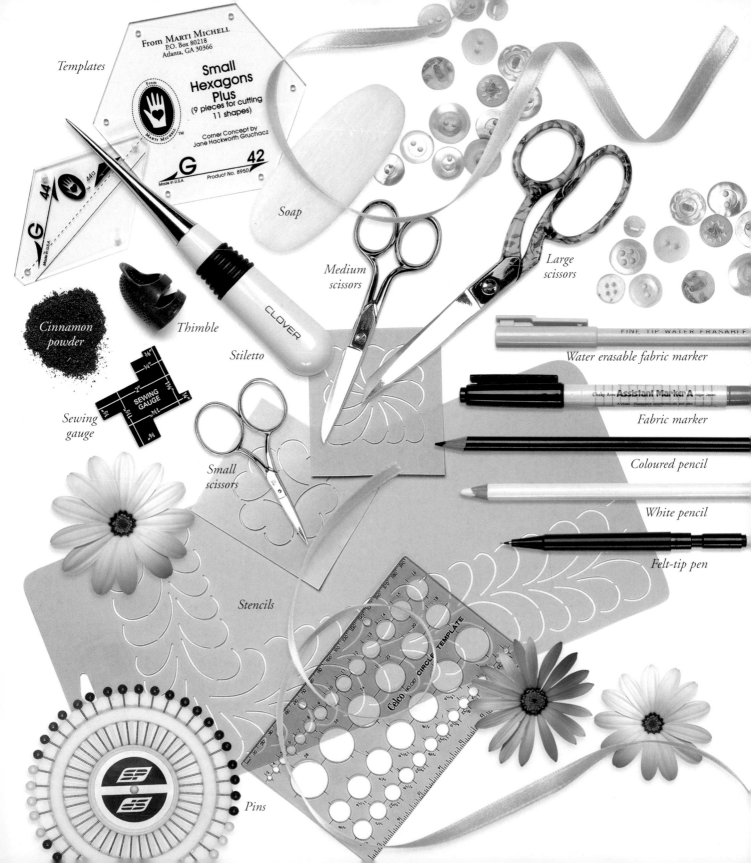

Templates

From Marti Michell
P.O. Box 80218
Atlanta, GA 30366

Small
Hexagons
Plus
(9 pieces for cutting
11 shapes)

Corner Concept by
Jane Hackworth Gruchacz

G 42

Made in U.S.A.   Product No. 8950

Soap

Medium
scissors

Large
scissors

CLOVER

Water erasable fabric marker

FINE TIP WATER ERASABLE

Cinnamon
powder

Thimble

Assistant Marker A

Fabric marker

Stiletto

SEWING
GAUGE

Sewing
gauge

Coloured pencil

White pencil

Small
scissors

Felt-tip pen

Stencils

Celco CIRCLE TEMPLATE

Pins

use. You must be able to comfortably hold the needle under the centre of the hoop with your elbow bent. Ensure the hoop has enough depth to hold the layers of fabric firmly.

Smaller hoops are also a valuable aid for surface embroidery and beading.

Frames

Frames for quilting can vary from small hand held frames, that are used in a similar manner to a hoop, to large floor frames which hold an entire quilt. They are generally less maneuverable than hoops.

Needles

Needles come in a variety of shapes and sizes. The size of a needle is given as a number. For hand sewing needles, the higher the number, the finer the needle. For machine sewing needles, the smaller the number, the finer the needle.

Both machine and hand sewing needles dull with use.

Hand sewing needles

Betweens - also known as quilting needles, are very short needles with small round eyes. Use for quilting by hand. Sizes 8 - 12 are the most commonly used by quilters.

Sharps - are medium length needles with small round eyes. Use for general hand sewing, appliqué and piecing by hand.

Darners - long thick needles with a large eye. Use for basting.

Crewel needles - are medium length needles with a large, elongated eye and are very easy to thread. Use for surface embroidery.

Straw or milliner's needles - are long slender needles with a small eye. Use for appliqué, knot embroidery and beading.

Beading needles - are long, very thin needles with a small eye. Use for stringing beads.

Chenille needles - are short, thick needles with large, elongated eyes. Use for thicker threads or multiple threads in surface embroidery.

Tapestry needles - are short and thick with elongated eyes and blunt tips. Use for some surface embroidery techniques and corded quilting.

Machine sewing needles

The most common machine sewing needle is a universal. For woven fabrics a sharp tipped needle is required.

Generally use as small a needle as the thread you are using will allow.

Twin and triple needles are also available and these can be used for channel or grid quilting.

Thimbles

A thimble is an invaluable tool for hand quilting. Even if you have shied away from wearing a thimble for other forms of needlework it is worth reconsidering for quilting.

Choose a thimble that fits your finger snugly and comfortably and one that allows you to push the needle with the ball and pad of your finger, not the very tip. When you have several stitches stacked onto the needle it requires considerable pressure to push the needle through the fabric, so ensure the thimble you select is very sturdy. Metal thimbles are the safest option here.

The tiny dimples in the end of a thimble are designed to hold the end of the needle so it does not slip away as you push. Ensure the dimples are deep enough to do this job and not simply window dressing.

The other consideration is the length of your fingernails. Flat topped thimbles will exert pressure on even the shortest nails. Fortunately today, there are several options available that have an opening to better accommodate your fingernail no matter what length it may be.

Other tools

Seam rippers - are useful for unpicking both hand sewn and machined stitches. Choose one that has a protective cover over the blade and feels comfortable in your hand.

Needle threaders - are helpful if you are having trouble threading a hand held needle or if your sewing machine does not have a needle threading attachment.

Cotton gloves - If you are having trouble gripping the fabric when quilting by machine, try wearing cotton gloves. Some gloves are available with rubber tips on the fingers to provide even more grip.

Stilletos - can be used for marking designs.

See page 87 for further information.

Pressing and starching

Pressing is an integral part of creating a beautifully finished quilt. The surface of your ironing board needs to be firm enough not to stretch pieces of fabric when the weight of the iron is applied to them. A good quality steam iron will make the time you spend pressing more enjoyable and fruitful. Pure cotton fabrics require a very high heat to press them adequately.

Press your fabrics before you even cut into them to ensure they are smooth and free from wrinkles and creases.

If some or all of your fabrics feel limp, apply spray starch to give them more body. However, it is more difficult to hand quilt starched fabric than unstarched fabric, so consider the techniques you intend to use before applying too much starch.

All seam allowances need to be pressed before sewing an adjoining seam. Wherever possible, press a seam allowance towards the darker of two fabrics. If this isn't possible, trim the darker seam allowance so it is slightly narrower than the lighter one. First, press the stitching while the two layers of fabric are still together to meld and set the stitches. Then open out the fabric and press the seam from the right side.

If several seams meet at the same point, press the seams open instead of to one side. Press these seams from the wrong side of the fabric. This will help to reduce bulk at these points.

To minimise the risk of stretching fabric pieces, use a press and lift action with the iron rather than gliding it across the fabric. Where a seam joins two pieces of fabric, one along the straight grain and one along the bias grain, keep the iron over the piece of fabric with the seam on the straight grain in preference to the other piece of fabric. Avoid pressing unstitched edges that are cut on the bias. If this is not possible, definitely do not apply steam to these edges.

Caring for your quilt

Laundering

The gentlest way to clean a quilt is to vacuum it at least every six months. Lay the quilt out flat on a clean sheet or similar and vacuum both sides using a soft upholstery nozzle on the vacuum cleaner.

If a quilt requires further cleaning, there are several options available depending on what materials were used to make the quilt.

For a pure cotton quilt, gently hand wash it in your bathtub using a very mild soap powder or liquid. Rinse the quilt thoroughly, squeezing the water from the quilt between rinses. Never wring the quilt. After the final squeezing, roll the quilt in towelling to remove as much water as possible and then lay it out flat to dry.

Drycleaning is the most appropriate method to use for quilts made from silk and wool. Ensure your chosen cleaner is experienced with this type of work before committing your precious quilt to their care.

If your quilt has been made with machine washable fabrics, machine wash it using the gentlest settings on your machine. Dry in the same manner as a hand washed quilt.

Storing

The very best way to store a quilt is to lay it out flat on a bed! Cover the quilt if you need to protect it from strong light.

The next best alternative is to roll the quilt onto a tube with layers of acid free tissue paper between the layers. The third choice is to fold the quilt, again placing acid free tissue paper between the layers, and store the quilt in an archive box or cloth bag. To prevent permanent creases forming, refold the quilt every few weeks. Likewise, acid free tissue paper needs to be replaced approximately every three years, as its beneficial effects gradually diminish over time.

Sizes of quilts

Before beginning your quilt, you will need to determine the finished size. If the quilt is to go onto a bed the following chart is a useful guide.

Comforter - the quilt lies on the top of a mattress with no overhang and pillows are placed on top of the quilt.

Coverlet - the quilt covers the sides of the mattress and the pillows.

Bedspread - the quilt reaches almost to the floor and covers the pillows.

If you have a specific bed in mind, measure this bed as mattress sizes can vary. For a quilt that is to be used as a coverlet or bedspread, add approximately 30cm (12") to the length of the mattress and overhang at the end. This enables the quilt to adequately cover the pillows and be tucked under them.

QUILT SIZE GUIDE

Bed	Mattress	Comforter	Coverlet	Bedpsread
		No allowance for pillow tuck or overhang	30cm (12") allowance for pillow tuck and 32cm (13") allowance for overhang	30cm (12") allowance for pillow tuck and 52cm (21") allowance for overhang
Cot	115cm x 57cm wide 46" x 23" wide	115cm x 57cm wide 46" x 23" wide	150cm x 100cm wide 60" x 40" wide	Not applicable
Single or Twin	187cm x 98cm wide 75" x 39" wide	187cm x 98cm wide 75" x 39" wide	249cm x 162cm wide 98" x 64" wide	269cm x 212cm wide 106" x 84" wide
Double	187cm x 137cm wide 74" x 54" wide	187cm x 137cm wide 74" x 54" wide	249cm x 201cm wide 98" x 79" wide	269cm x 241cm wide 106" x 95" wide
Queen	200cm x 150cm wide 79" x 59" wide	200cm x 150cm wide 79" x 59" wide	262cm x 214cm wide 103" x 84" wide	282cm x 254cm wide 111" x 100" wide
King	210cm x 180cm wide 83" x 71" wide	210cm x 180cm wide 83" x 71" wide	272cm x 244cm wide 107" x 96" wide	292cm x 284cm wide 115" x 112" wide

Preparation

Those who sleep under a quilt,

sleep under a blanket of love.

Anonymous

Templates

The importance of making and using perfectly accurate templates cannot be stressed too much. They are the foundation stones of your pieced quilt and if they are just a little out, the effect will be magnified as you build up your entire quilt top. Always check the templates you make against the original pattern. If they do not align perfectly, discard them and make new ones.

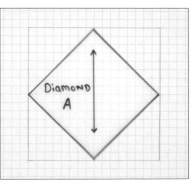

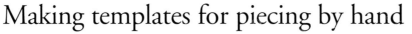

Making templates for piecing by hand

These templates are traditionally made without the seam allowances being included.

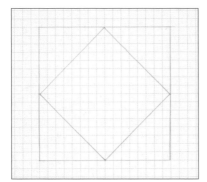

1. Draw your desired pattern accurately onto grid paper.

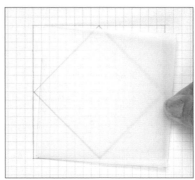

2. Place a piece of template plastic over a pattern piece (or this could be a pattern piece in a magazine or book).

3. Using a very fine permanent marker, trace over the pattern.

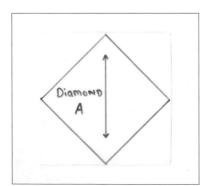

4. Label the template and mark the grain line as indicated on the pattern.

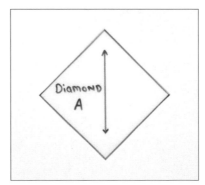

5. Using sharp scissors or a scalpel, carefully cut out the template along the marked outline.

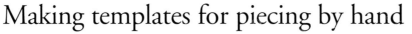

6. Place the template over the pattern piece to check its accuracy.

Making templates for piecing by machine

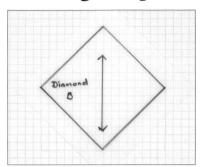

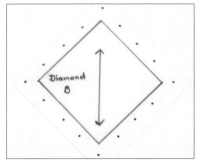

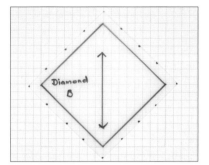

1. Follow steps 1 - 4 on the previous page.

2. Measure and mark a 6mm (¹/₄") seam allowance around the shape.

3. Carefully cut out and check the template following steps 5 and 6 on the previous page.

These templates include the seam allowances.

Using templates for piecing by hand

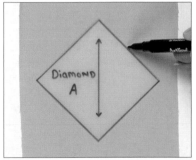

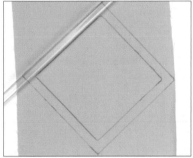

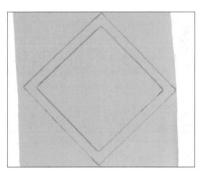

1. Position the template onto the wrong side of the pressed fabric, aligning the marked grain line with the grain of the fabric. Trace around the template.

2. Using a ruler to measure, or gauging the distance by eye, mark a 6mm (¹/₄") seam allowance around all sides of the shape.

3. Marked shape ready for cutting out.

preparation templates

....

15

Using templates for piecing by machine

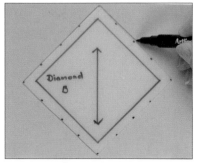

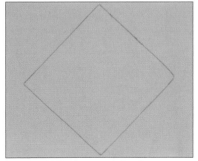

1. Position the template onto the wrong side of the pressed fabric, aligning the marked grain line with the grain of the fabric. Trace around the template.

2. Marked shape ready for cutting out.

3. Templates can be traced edge to edge so the shapes share a cutting line.

Cutting out

Fabric pieces can be cut out with either scissors or a rotary cutter. The rotary cutter, used in conjunction with a self-healing mat, makes it easier to achieve perfectly straight lines and accurately cut several layers of fabric at the one time. You can often do away with the need to make separate templates.

It is also much quicker to use than scissors, however it is not suitable for all shapes - curves and inside corners are often best cut with scissors.

Using a rotary cutter

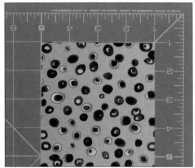

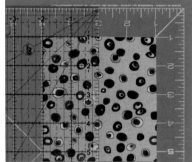

1. Press the fabric carefully to ensure there are no creases or wrinkles. Spread your fabric out on a self-healing mat, ensuring the grain of the fabric is aligned with the marked grid on the mat.

2. Position the ruler on the fabric where you wish to cut. For right handers, line up the right hand edge of the ruler with the position of the cutting line. For left handers, line up the left hand edge of the ruler with the position of the cutting line.

3. Holding the ruler firmly in place and starting at the edge closest to you, push the cutter along the edge of the ruler. Press firmly to ensure you cut cleanly.

Cutting strips

Cutting squares and rectangles

Cutting half-square triangles

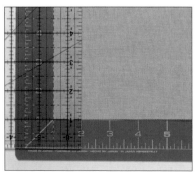

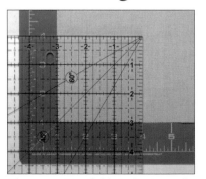

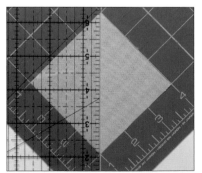

Place the ruler on the fabric so the required strip lies underneath the ruler. The cut edge of the fabric should align with a line on the ruler for its entire length.

Place a strip of fabric horizontally across the cutting mat. Ensure lines on the ruler line up with both the lower and side cut edges of the fabric.

Turn the cutting mat diagonally. Line up the square of fabric with the grid on the mat. Ensure the edge of the ruler is aligned with both the top and bottom corners of the square.

When cutting long strips, fold the fabric concertina fashion and cut across the folds through all layers at the same time.

Cutting quarter-square triangles

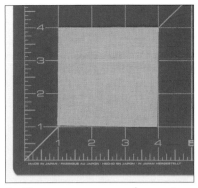

1. Cut a square, as on the previous page.

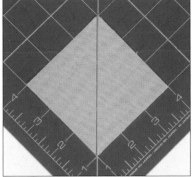

2. Reposition the mat, fabric and ruler as shown for half-square triangles. Cut the square diagonally to form two half-square triangles.

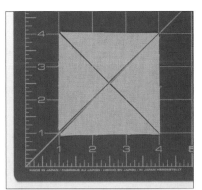

3. Without moving the fabric, turn the mat 90°. Place the ruler across the cut square from corner to corner. Cut to form four quarter-square triangles.

Cutting diamonds

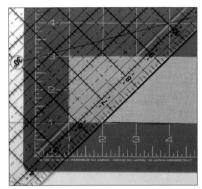

1. Place a strip of fabric horizontally across the cutting mat. Align the 45° or 60° line on the ruler with the lower edge of the strip and cut.

2. Move the ruler along the required distance, keeping the 45° or 60° line on the ruler aligned with the lower edge of the strip. Cut as before.

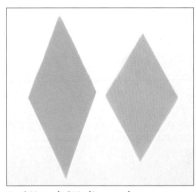

3. 45° and 60° diamonds.

CUTTING WITHOUT TEMPLATES

■ When cutting out shapes without using templates, add the following amounts to the sizes of finished shapes for the seam allowances.

■ **Squares and rectangles:** add 12mm ($1/2$") to the finished size.

■ **Half-square triangles:** add 22mm ($7/8$") to the finished size of the square.

■ **Quarter-square triangles:** add 32mm ($1 1/4$") to the finished size of the square.

Trimming points

Trimming the points from triangles, diamonds and the like can make piecing easier, particularly when piecing by machine.

Method 1

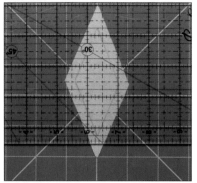

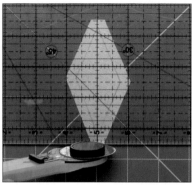

1. Place the fabric shape on the mat. Place the edge of the ruler exactly 6mm ($^1/4$") out from the finished point.

2. Cut. Place the edge of the ruler exactly 6mm ($^1/4$") out from the next finished point.

3. Cut. Repeat for any remaining points.

Method 2

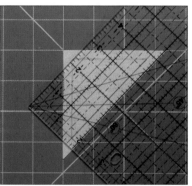

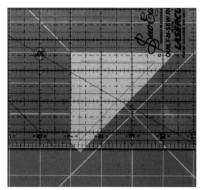

1. Place the fabric shape on the mat. Place the edge of the ruler exactly 6mm ($^1/4$") out from a finished point and at 90° to one of the intersecting lines that creates the point.

2. Cut. Place the edge of the ruler exactly 6mm ($^1/4$") out from the same finished point but at 90° to the other intersecting line that creates the point.

3. Cut. Repeat the procedure for each point.

HINTS ON CUTTING OUT

■ Whether using scissors or a rotary cutter, always ensure the fabric has been carefully pressed before cutting. Even the smallest crease or wrinkle can affect the accuracy of your fabric piece and this can have an adverse effect on the entire block.

Creating the
Quilt top

May your sorrows be patched and your joys quilted.

Anonymous

Pieced quilt tops have a long tradition and can be categorized according to how the designs are organized.

Many are made from repeating patchwork blocks, which use a grid of squares as the basis for the designs. These squares are further divided into other geometric shapes.

There are also numerous specialty patterns that are used to create regular blocks. Log cabin blocks begin with a central square which is surrounded with successive strips of fabric until it is the desired size. Flying geese designs utilize rows of triangles. Dresden plate designs form a circular design within the block.

There are several alternatives to these patchwork blocks. One-patch designs rely on the repetition of a single shape. Tumbling blocks, hexagons and diamonds are wonderful examples of this category.

Medallion quilts begin with a central square or rectangle which is surrounded with concentric frames. Pictorial and crazy patchwork quilts require piecing without necessarily relying on a regular block design.

A single piece of fabric can also be used to create a quilt top. Here the actual quilting usually dominates the design.

Appliqué is often used in the creation of quilt tops, whether they are created from blocks or are single piece quilt tops. Like patchwork, it can utilize hand and machine sewing techniques. Stained glass quilts, Hawaiian quilts, Baltimore Album quilts and broderie perse are wonderful examples of appliquéd quilts.

The needlework techniques that can be incorporated into a quilt top are only limited by your creativity and knowledge. Embellishing with embroidery and beading, both by hand and machine, can add a special something to ensure your quilt is unique. These enable you to include intricate details that you cannot achieve with fabric alone.

Numerous fabric manipulation techniques, such as pleating, tucking, ruching and gathering can add further dimension to a quilt top.

One-patch designs

Tumbling blocks

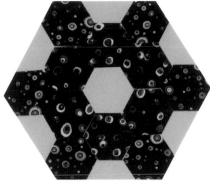
Hexagons

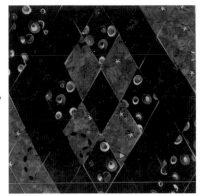
Diamonds

Four-patch blocks

These are made up of a grid that can be divided by four.

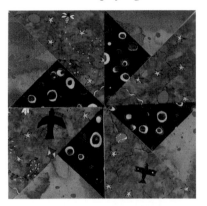

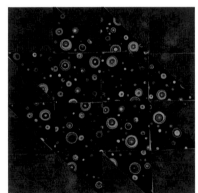

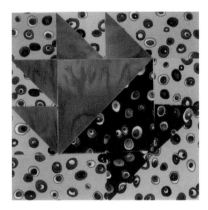

Five-patch blocks

These are made up of a grid that is five squares across and five squares deep. A block contains 25 equal units.

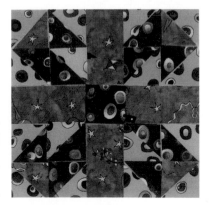

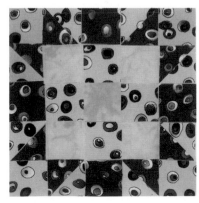

Seven-patch blocks

These are made up of a grid that is seven squares across and seven squares deep. A block contains 49 equal units.

Nine-patch blocks

These are made up of a grid that can be divided by three.

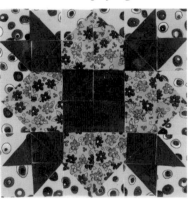 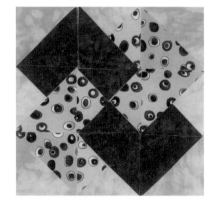 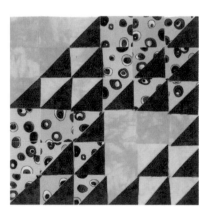

Specialty designs

Flying geese

Log cabin

Rail fence

Piecing by hand Straight seam

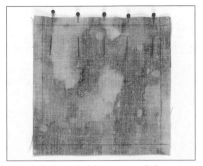 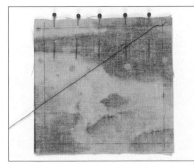 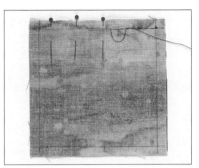

1. Mark the stitchline around the outer edge of each piece. Place right sides together and match stitchlines. Pin the pieces together at 2.5cm (1") intervals and exactly at the marked corners.

2. Secure the thread with a back stitch exactly at the marked corner (the corner on the right hand side for right handers and the corner on the left hand side for left handers).

3. Using small running stitches (approximately 8 stitches to the inch or 2.5cm), begin stitching along the marked stitchline.

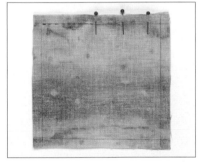 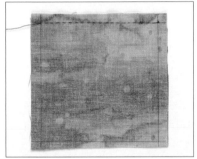 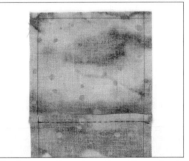

4. Check the back to ensure the stitches go through both marked stitchlines. If they do not, remove the stitches and re-align the stitchlines.

5. Removing the pins as you go, stitch to the end of the marked stitchline.

6. Secure the thread with a back stitch and trim. Press.

Butted seam

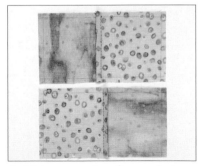 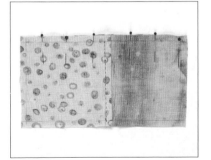 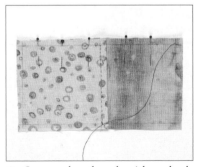

1. Make two pairs of seamed pieces following the instructions above. Open out each pair and press the seams to one side, pressing them in opposite directions.

2. Place two pairs, right sides together and match marked stitchlines. Pin the pieces together at 2.5cm (1") intervals and exactly at the marked corners and butted seam.

3. Secure the thread with a back stitch exactly at the marked corner (the corner on the right hand side for right handers and the corner on the left hand side for left handers).

Butted seam *continued*

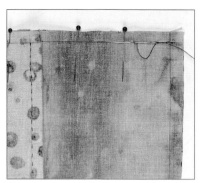

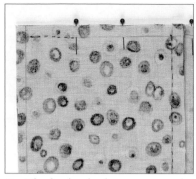

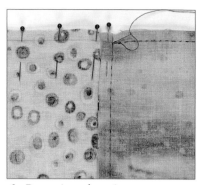

4. Using small running stitches (approximately 8 stitches to the inch or 2.5cm), begin stitching along the marked stitchline.

5. Check the back to ensure the stitches go through both marked stitchlines. If they do not, remove the stitches and re-align the stitchlines.

6. Removing the pins as you go, stitch to the pin at the butted seam. Do not stitch through the seam allowance, push it out of the way towards the unstitched section.

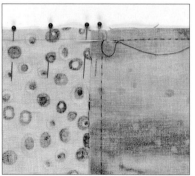

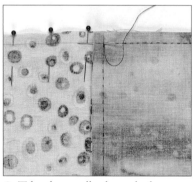

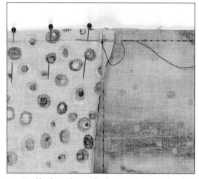

7. Remove the pin. Work a back stitch at the marked corner next to the butted seam.

8. Take the needle through the seam allowance.

9. Pull the thread through. Push the seam allowance back towards the previous stitching. Work a back stitch at the marked corner.

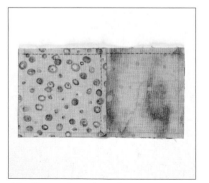

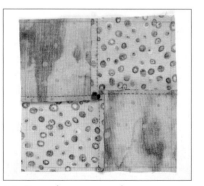

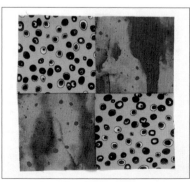

10. Removing the pins as you go, stitch to the end of the marked stitchline. Secure the thread with a back stitch and trim.

11. Press the seams as shown.

12. Right side of fabric.

Set in seam

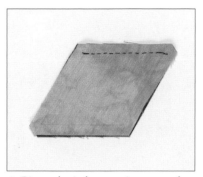

1. Pin and stitch two pieces together following the instructions for a straight seam.

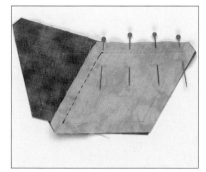

2. With right sides together and carefully matching the marked stitchlines, place a third piece onto the first piece. Placing pins at right angles to the stitchline, pin the pieces together at 2.5cm (1") intervals and exactly at the marked corners.

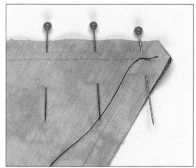

3. Secure the thread with a back stitch exactly at the marked corner (the corner on the right hand side for right handers and the corner on the left hand side for left handers).

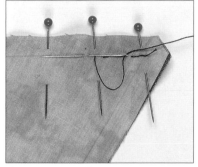

4. Using small running stitches (approximately 8 stitches to the inch or 2.5cm), begin stitching along the marked stitchline.

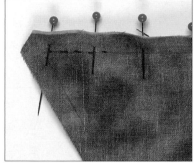

5. Check the back to ensure the stitches go through both marked stitchlines. If they do not, remove the stitches and re-align the stitchlines.

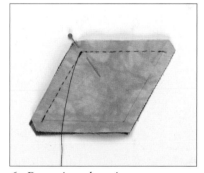

6. Removing the pins as you go, stitch to the pin at the corner. Ensure the seam allowance on the first piece is out of the way.

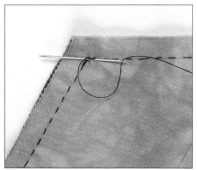

7. Remove the pin. Work a back stitch at the marked corner next to the end of the previous seam.

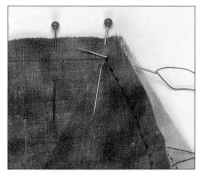

8. Pivot the third piece at the corner. Pin the adjacent side to the second piece. Ensure stitchlines match. Take needle through the seam allowance.

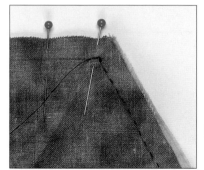

9. Secure the thread with a back stitch exactly at the marked corner.

Set in seam *continued*

10. Stitch along this side in the same manner as before, finishing with a back stitch at the corner.

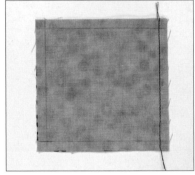

11. Press the seams flat.

12. Right side of fabric.

Piecing by machine Straight seam

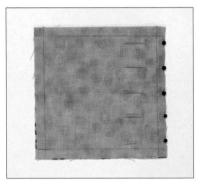

1. Place two pieces right sides together, carefully matching raw edges. Placing pins at right angles to the stitchline, pin the pieces together.

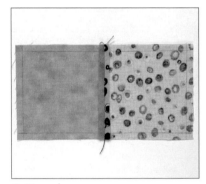

2. Using a machine straight stitch and leaving a 6mm (1/4") seam allowance, stitch from edge to edge.

3. Press the seam open.

QUILTING THROUGH THE AGES

■ Quilting has a rich tradition in many societies around the world.
Egyptian tombs and archaeological digs along the Silk Road between India and China have yielded evidence of quilting that dates back over 5,000 years.

■ It is believed that quilting first came to Europe from the East during the time of the Crusades. In Europe it was initially used to make garments that were used in battle as the quilting lessened the impact of weapons. With the development of metal armour, quilted garments were worn to protect the wearer from chafing from the armour.

■ It appears that quilting first became used in English homes - for both clothing and bedding - during the sixteenth century. It continued to grown in popularity and was particularly widespread during the eighteenth century.

Chain piecing

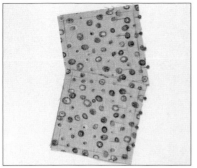

1. Pin pairs of pieces together, following step 1 on the previous page.

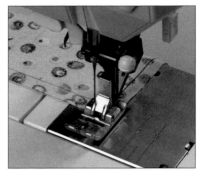

2. Stitch along one side of the first pinned pair, following step 2 on the previous page. Take 2 - 3 more stitches beyond the edge of the pieces.

3. Without lifting the presser foot, begin to feed a second pinned pair under the foot.

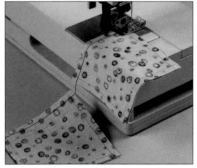

4. Stitch the seam on this pair in the same manner. Take 2 - 3 more stitches beyond the edge of the pieces.

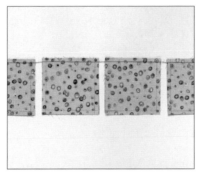

5. Continue stitching pieces in the same manner until the desired number are complete.

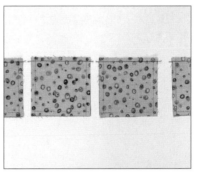

6. Cut the stitching between the pairs to separate them.

Butted seam

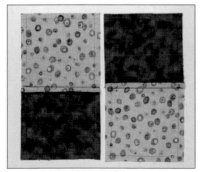

1. Make two pairs of seamed pieces following steps 1 and 2 on the previous page. Press the seams flat, ensuring the seam allowances face in opposite directions.

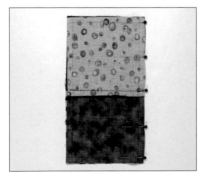

2. With right sides together and matching raw edges and seams, pin the two seamed pieces together. Ensure the pins are at right angles to the stitchline.

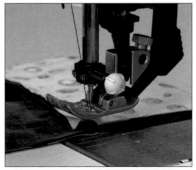

3. Using a machine straight stitch, stitch up to the butted seams. Finish with the needle in the down position. Lift the presser foot and recheck that the seams are aligned.

Butted seam *continued*

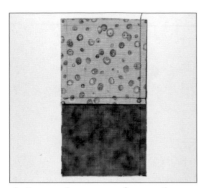

4. Lower the presser foot and continue stitching to the end.

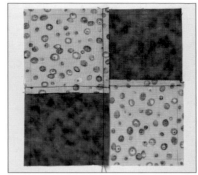

5. Press the seams flat.

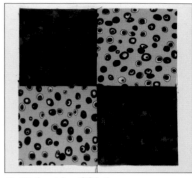

6. Right side of fabric.

Set in seam

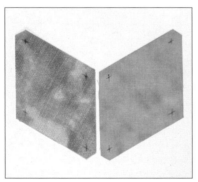

1. On the wrong side of each piece, mark the seam allowances at the corners.

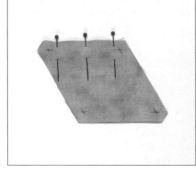

2. Place two pieces right sides together, ensuring the markings are aligned. Pin, placing the pins at right angles to the stitchline.

3. Starting and finishing at the marked corners, and securing the thread at the beginning and end, stitch the seam with a machine straight stitch.

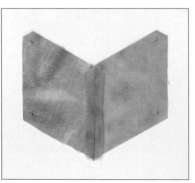

4. Press the seam open.

5. With right sides together, pin the third piece to the first two pieces in the same manner as in step 2.

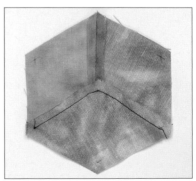

6. Stitch from corner mark to corner mark, pivoting at the seam. Press.

Sewing curves

1. Transfer all matching marks as well as stitchlines to the wrong sides of the pieces.

2. With right sides together and matching all markings, pin the two pieces together with the convex curve on the top. Place the pins at right angles to the stitchline.

3. Secure the thread with a back stitch exactly at the marked corner.

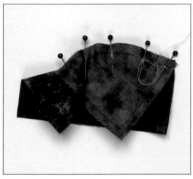

4. Using small running stitches (approximately 8 stitches to the inch or 2.5cm), begin stitching along the marked stitchline.

5. Check the back to ensure the stitches go through both marked stitchlines. If they do not, remove the stitches and re-align the stitch lines.

6. Removing the pins as you go, stitch to the end of the marked stitchline.

7. Secure the thread with a back stitch and trim.

8. Press the seam allowance. If necessary, clip the seam allowance to ensure it lies flat.

9. Right side of fabric.

The same procedure is used for piecing by both hand and machine.

Foundation piecing

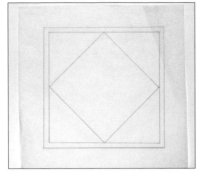

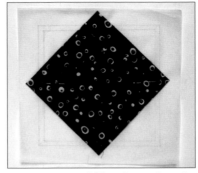

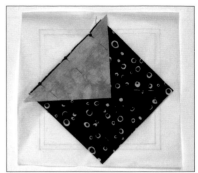

1. Transfer the block pattern to fabric stabilizer or semi-transparent paper such as baking paper. Cut out the foundation beyond the marked outer edge of the block.

2. Cut a piece of fabric larger than the first shape. With the right side uppermost, position it onto the wrong side of the foundation. Ensure it overlaps all marked stitchlines by at least 6mm (1/4"). Pin in place.

3. Cut a second piece of fabric large enough to cover the second shape plus seam allowances. With right sides together, pin it to the first piece.

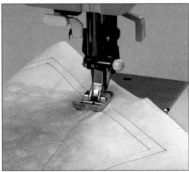

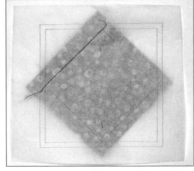

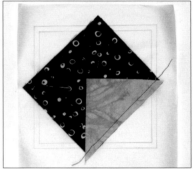

4. Using a large needle (size 90/14 is good), position the foundation and fabric pieces under the presser foot, foundation side up.

5. Using tiny machine straight stitches and starting and finishing 6mm (1/4") beyond the ends of the marked stitchline, stitch through all three layers.

6. Turn the foundation over and trim the seam allowance to 6mm (1/4").

Foundation piecing makes it easier to accurately sew difficult to piece blocks. Use a larger needle than normal.

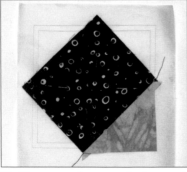

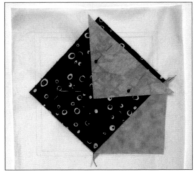

7. Open out the second piece and press it flat against the foundation.

8. Cut a piece of fabric large enough to cover the third shape plus seam allowances. With right sides together, pin this piece in place as before.

9. With the foundation uppermost, stitch in the same manner as before.

Foundation piecing *continued*

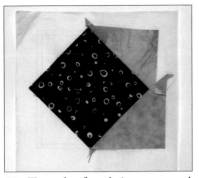

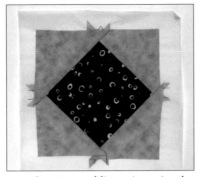

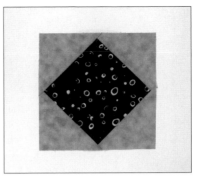

10. Turn the foundation over and trim the seam allowance to 6mm (1/4"). Open out the third piece and press it flat against the foundation.

11. Continue adding pieces in the same manner until the entire block is covered, trimming seam allowances and pressing after each addition.

12. Trim the pieced fabric and foundation to the exact size plus seam allowances. Remove the foundation after the block has been joined to other blocks.

Strip piecing

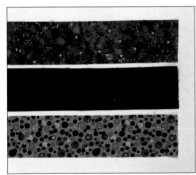

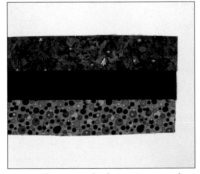

1. Cut strips of fabric. Ensure the grain of the fabric lies in the same direction for each piece.

2. Machine stitch the strips together along the long edges, following the instructions on page 26.

3. Make more than one set of strips.

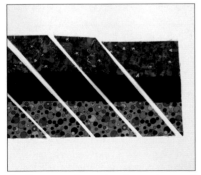

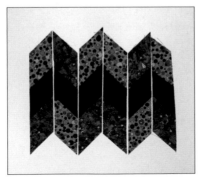

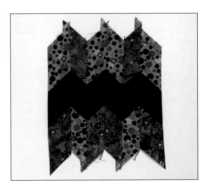

4. Crosscut the strips into pieces of the desired shape and size.

5. Re-arrange pieces to form your design.

6. Join the pieces together following the instructions on pages 26 - 28 for piecing by machine.

Strip piecing is useful for creating diamonds and is a quicker and easier method than cutting out each piece individually.

English piecing

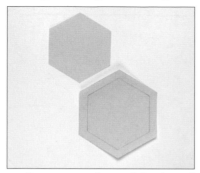

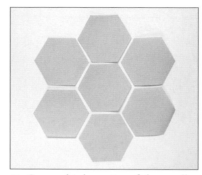

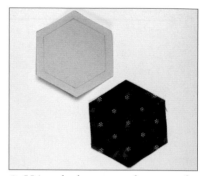

1. Cut two templates of the desired shape - one the exact size of the finished patches and one with the seam allowance added.

2. Cut multiple copies of the smaller template from paper. You will need a separate template for each patch.

3. Using the larger template, transfer the shape onto your chosen fabrics. Ensure the grain of the fabric always runs in the same direction on each patch. Cut out the patches.

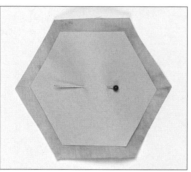

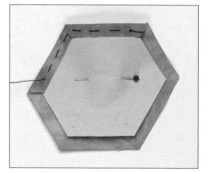

4. Centre a paper template onto the wrong side of a fabric patch and pin in place.

5. Fold over the seam allowance along one side, ensuring it is snug against the template. Tack in place.

6. Fold over the seam allowance on the next side in the same manner, ensuring the corner is sharp. Tack as before.

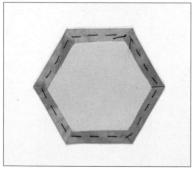

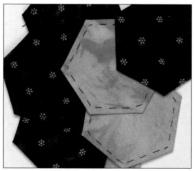

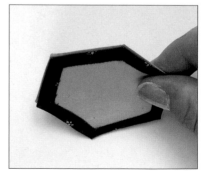

7. Continue around the entire shape in the same manner.

8. Repeat the procedure for the required number of patches.

9. Place two patches right sides together, ensuring the edges match exactly. Thread a needle with quilting thread.

English piecing *continued*

10. Take the needle behind the seam allowance of one patch and emerge at the corner.

11. Using tiny overcast stitches, stitch the two patches together along one side. Work several stitches back over the previous stitching for a short distance and end off the thread.

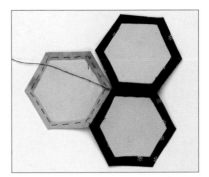

12. Attach a third patch to the first in the same manner. With right sides together, stitch the third patch to the next side of the first patch.

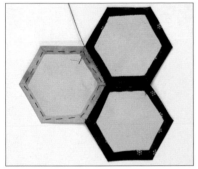

13. Reposition the third patch so it is right sides together with the adjacent side of the second patch. Stitch as before and end off the thread.

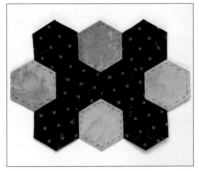

14. Continue attaching patches in the same manner. When several patches are sewn together, press them flat.

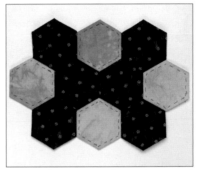

15. Only remove the tacking and paper template when all sides of the shape have been stitched to other patches or an edging.

Log cabin

1. Cut out the centre square or other geometric shape. Cut strips, all the same width, from your selected fabrics.

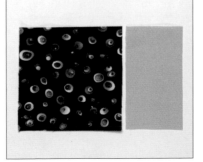

2. Cut a piece of one strip the same length as one side of the square.

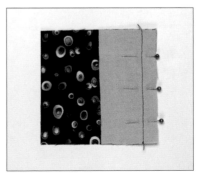

3. With right sides together, pin and stitch the strip to the square.

creating the quilt top patchwork and piecing

....

33

The log cabin block is one of the simplest blocks to make and is a good way to use up scraps of fabric. Any straight sided geometric shape can form the centrepiece.

Log cabin *continued*

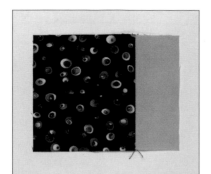

4. Press the seam open so that the strip lies flat.

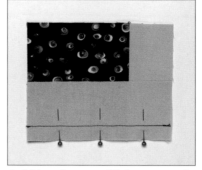

5. Using the same fabric, cut a strip the length of the square plus the first strip. With right sides together, pin and stitch the strip to the square and end of the first strip.

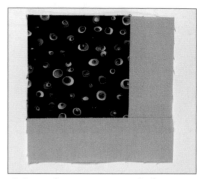

6. Press the seam open as before.

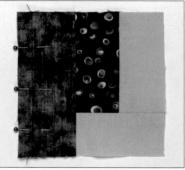

7. Using a contrasting fabric, cut a strip the same length as the previous strip. With right sides together, pin and stitch the strip to the square and end of the second strip.

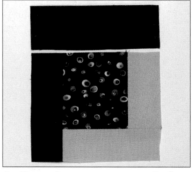

8. Press the seam open as before. Using the same fabric as the last strip, cut a piece long enough to fit along the fourth side of the square and attached strips.

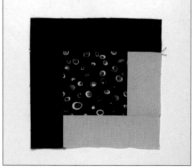

9. With right sides together, pin and stitch. Press the seam open as before.

10. Cut a strip the same length as the first side. With right sides together, pin and stitch. Press the seam open as before.

11. Working in a clockwise direction, add three more strips in the same manner to complete the round.

12. Continue in the same manner until the block is the desired size.

Crazy patchwork - method one (raw edges)

1. Cut a piece of foundation fabric to the desired size. Cut out the first shape for the centre (shapes with five or more sides work particularly well).

2. With right sides uppermost, fuse or pin the shape to the foundation fabric.

3. Place a second shape onto the foundation fabric so it slightly overlaps the first shape. Allow a 6mm (1/4") overlap if pinning and less if fusing.

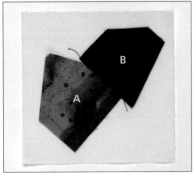

4. If pinning, baste the second shape along the edge that overlaps the first shape, stitching through all layers.

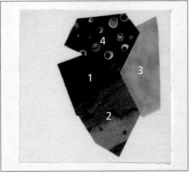

5. Working around the first shape in an anti-clockwise direction, position a third and then a fourth shape, securing as before.

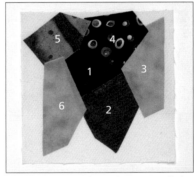

6. Continue adding shapes until the first shape is completely enclosed.

7. Continue working in rounds until the foundation fabric is completely covered.

8. Trim away any sections of fabric that overhang the edge of the foundation fabric.

9. Work surface embroidery along each seamline (see pages 67 - 73 for embroidery stitch instructions).

Crazy patchwork - method two (turned edges)

1. Cut a piece of foundation fabric to the desired size. Cut out the first shape for the centre (shapes with five or more sides work particularly well).

2. With right sides uppermost, pin the centre shape to the foundation fabric.

3. With right sides together and aligning one edge, place a second shape onto the first shape. Pin and stitch through all three layers.

4. Flip the second shape back so its right side is uppermost. Press the seam and pin to the foundation fabric.

5. Trim the ends of the shape even with the first shape.

6. With right sides together, position a third shape along the edge created by the first two shapes.

7. Pin and stitch as before.

8. Flip the third shape back so its right side is uppermost. Press the seam and pin to the foundation fabric. Trim the ends of the shape even with the previous shapes.

9. Continue adding shapes in the same manner until the first shape is completely enclosed.

Crazy patchwork method 2 *continued*

10. Continue working in rounds until the foundation fabric is completely covered.

11. Trim away any sections of fabric that overhang the edge of the foundation fabric.

12. Work surface embroidery along each seamline (see pages 67 - 73 for embroidery stitch instructions).

Seminole patchwork

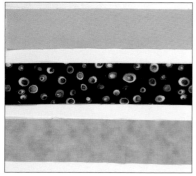

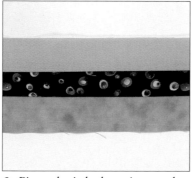

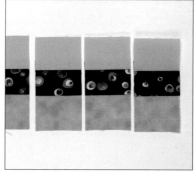

1. Cut several strips of contrasting fabrics, each 4cm (1 1/2") wide.

2. Pin and stitch the strips together along their long edges, using a 6mm (1/4") seam allowance. Press.

3. Cut the strips into 3.5cm (1 3/8") pieces.

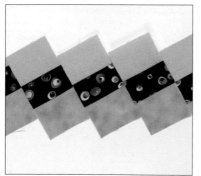

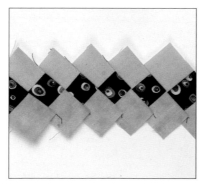

4. Reposition the pieces. Here we have moved each piece across by the width of one strip.

5. Pin and stitch the pieces together to form one long band.

6. Attach a long strip of contrasting fabric along each side of the band.

Seminole patchwork was created by the Seminole Indians of the south-east of North America. A wide variety of designs can be created, depending on the way the strips are cut.

■ Before cutting out all the pieces you require, make a test block to see if you like the selected fabrics together. This is also a good check for the accuracy of the pattern you are using.

■ Take extra care to ensure your seams are accurately stitched. Any inaccuracies magnify as you progress with your quilt top.

■ Wherever possible, press seam allowances towards the darker of two fabrics. If you need to press towards the lighter fabric, trim the seam allowance on the darker fabric to ensure it is slightly narrower than the seam allowance on the lighter fabric.

■ Study your block pattern to determine the simplest sewing order. Many patterns will indicate a sewing order by showing those pieces that should be joined first as lying closer together, grading to those that should be joined last as lying farthest apart.

Preparing appliqué shapes
Using paper-backed fusible web (or appliqué paper)

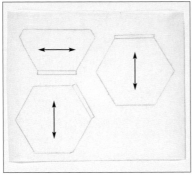

1. Trace or draw the exact outlines of the shapes onto the paper side of the fusible web. Where edges are overlapped by a second shape, add a 4mm (3/16") extension.

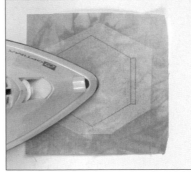

2. Roughly cut out the shapes and position them, paper side up, on the wrong side of the fabric. Ensure the grain of the fabric is correctly aligned. Using a press and lift action with the iron, fuse in place.

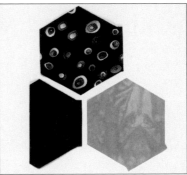

3. Cut out each piece along the marked outline and remove the backing paper.

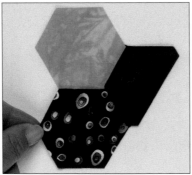

4. With right sides uppermost, position the shapes onto the background fabric. Ensure that all underlaps are completely covered.

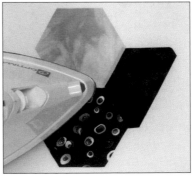

5. Again using a press and lift action with the iron, fuse the shapes to the background fabric.

6. The pieces are now ready to be appliquéd in place using your chosen method.

Using templates - method one

1. Trace or draw the exact outline of the shape onto template plastic. Add any markings.

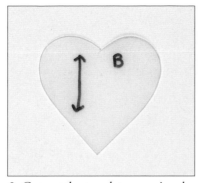

2. Cut out the template, ensuring the edges are smooth. This becomes your master template.

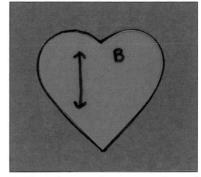

3. Place the template onto a piece of thin card or freezer paper and trace around it.

4. Carefully cut out the template from the card. If the same shape is to be used more than once, make a separate template from card for each time the shape is used in the design.

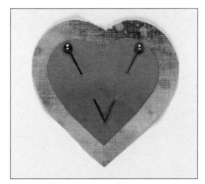

5. With wrong sides uppermost, pin the card template to the fabric. Cut out the shape from the fabric, including a 6mm (1/4") seam allowance.

6. Apply starch to the seam allowance, until it is quite damp.

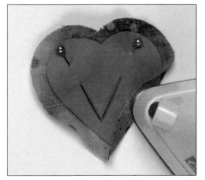

7. Beginning on a straight or gently curved side, press the seam allowance back over the template with the tip of the iron. Hold the iron in place until the fabric is dry.

8. When pressing the seam allowance of an outside curve, press small pleats into the turned seam allowance.

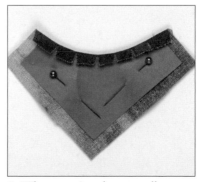

9. When pressing the seam allowance of an inside curve, clip the seam allowance at intervals. Make the cuts slightly shorter than the width of the seam allowance.

············

39

Using templates - method one *continued*

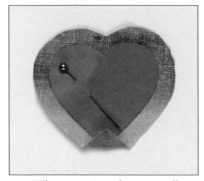

10. When pressing the seam allowance around an inside corner, clip into the corner in the same manner as an inside curve.

11. When pressing the seam allowance around an outside corner, first fold over the fabric at the tip.

12. Fold over the seam allowance along one side and press.

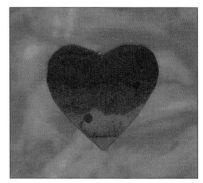

13. Fold over the seam allowance on the opposite side and press.

14. Continue around the shape until all of the seam allowance is pressed over the template, except for edges that underlap other pieces.

15. Just before you are ready to attach the shape, carefully remove the cardboard. With right sides uppermost, position the shape on the background fabric. Attach using your chosen appliqué method.

HINTS ON APPLIQUÉ

■ Cut the background or foundation fabric about 25mm (1") larger than is required in case the application of the appliqué 'shrinks' the fabric. It can be recut to the correct size once the appliqué is complete.

■ Mark lengthwise and crosswise centre lines on the background fabric to help you centre a design more accurately. These also help you to position the appliqué in the same place on multiple blocks that use the same design.

■ Wherever possible, the grain of all fabric pieces should run in the same direction.

■ Ensure the fabrics you combine have similar laundering requirements.

■ If the appliqué design utilizes overlapping motifs, cut out all motifs and position them on the fabric. Ensure they are layered correctly and number each piece in the order they need to be attached.

Using templates - method two (for circular shapes only)

1. Draw or trace the shape onto card or freezer paper. Cut out the template, ensuring the edges are smooth.

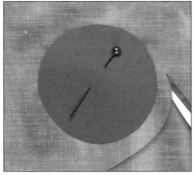

2. With wrong sides uppermost, pin the card template to the fabric. Cut out the shape from the fabric, including a 6mm ($^1/4$") seam allowance.

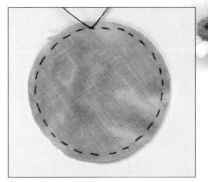

3. Remove the template. Using doubled thread, work running stitch around the shape 3mm ($^1/8$") from the cut edge. Do not end off the thread.

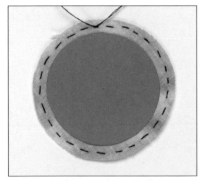

4. Centre the template on the wrong side of the fabric.

5. Pull up the running stitches to gather the seam allowance. Tie off the thread securely.

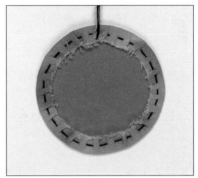

6. Steam press or starch and press the fabric.

7. Carefully remove the gathering thread and the template.

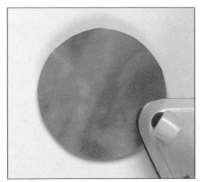

8. With the right side uppermost, carefully press the shape again.

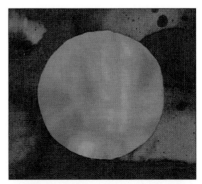

9. With right sides uppermost, position the shape on the background fabric and attach using your chosen appliqué method.

creating the quilt top appliqué

....

41

Hand appliqué Blanket stitch

1. Cut out the shape and apply it to the right side of the background fabric using your chosen method (see pages 38 - 41).

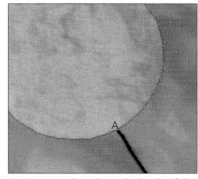

2. Secure a thread on the back of the background fabric. Bring it to the front at A, just next to the edge of the shape.

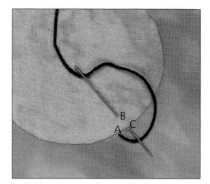

3. Take the needle to the back at B, within the shape. Re-emerge at C, just next to the edge of the shape. Ensure the thread is under the tip of the needle.

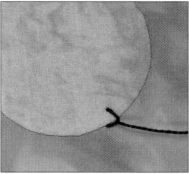

4. Pull the thread through until the stitch lies snugly against the edge of the shape but does not distort it.

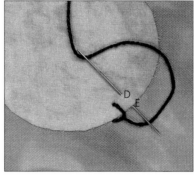

5. Take the needle to the back at D, within the shape. Re-emerge at E, just next to the edge of the shape. Ensure the thread is under the tip of the needle.

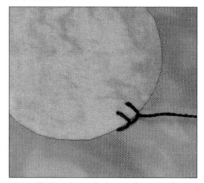

6. Pull the thread through as before.

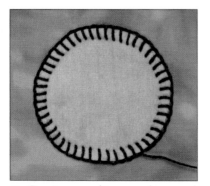

7. Continue working evenly spaced stitches around the shape in the same manner.

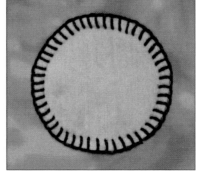

8. To finish, take the needle to the back of the fabric, where it first emerged. End off on the back of the fabric.

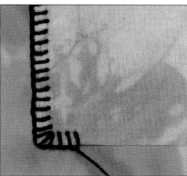

9. When turning a corner, keep the ends of the spokes very close together or even use the same hole. Maintain the stitch spacing at the outer edge.

Slip stitch

1. Cut out the shape, leaving a small seam allowance. Prepare and apply the shape to the right side of the background fabric using your chosen method (see pages 39 - 41). Ensure the seam allowance is turned under.

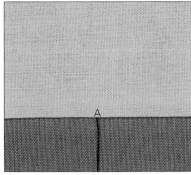

2. Secure a thread on the back of the background fabric. Bring it to the front at A, just next to the edge of the shape.

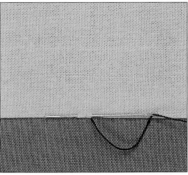

3. Take the needle behind the folded edge of the shape. Re-emerge a short distance away.

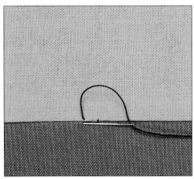

4. Pull the thread through. Take the needle to the back of the fabric, through the background fabric only.

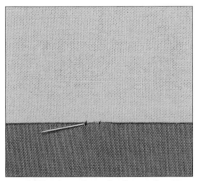

5. Pull the thread through. Re-emerge a short distance away, just next to the edge of the shape.

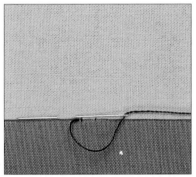

6. Pull the thread through. Again, take the needle behind the folded edge of the shape. Re-emerge a short distance away.

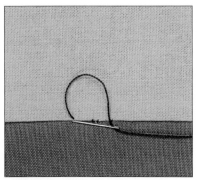

7. Pull the thread through. Take the needle to the back of the fabric as before.

8. Continue working stitches in the same manner around the entire edge of the shape.

9. To finish, end off the thread on the back of the fabric behind the shape.

creating the quilt top appliqué

....

43

Stab stitch

1. Cut out the shape, leaving a small seam allowance. Prepare and apply it to the right side of the background fabric using your chosen method (see pages 39 - 41). Ensure the seam allowance is turned under.

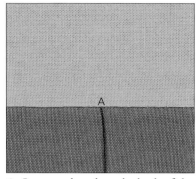

2. Secure a thread on the back of the background fabric. Bring it to the front at A, just next to the edge of the shape.

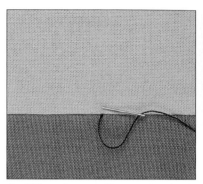

3. Take the needle to the back through the shape, but as close as possible to the folded edge.

4. Pull the thread through. Re-emerge a short distance away, just next to the edge of the shape.

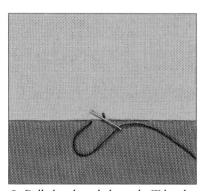

5. Pull the thread through. Take the needle to the back of the fabric as before.

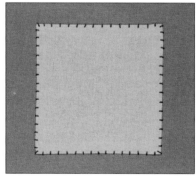

6. Pull the thread through. Continue working stitches in the same manner around the entire edge of the shape. To finish, end off the thread on the back of the fabric behind the shape.

HINTS ON APPLIQUÉ

■ When using blanket stitch, keep the spokes of the stitches at right angles to the edge of the shape at all times.

■ When appliquéing by machine, use a clear presser foot or open-toed appliqué presser foot so you can see exactly where you are sewing.

■ Hand appliqué may be worked using a hoop. This makes it easier to ensure that the foundation fabric does not become distorted.

Needle-turn appliqué

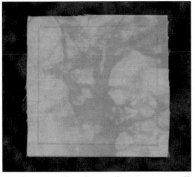

1. Cut out the shape, leaving a small seam allowance. Ensure the exact shape outline is marked on the right side of both the background fabric and the shape.

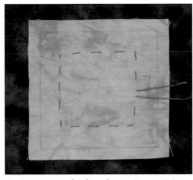

2. Pin or tack the shape in position, securing it with pins or stitches approximately 12mm ($^{1}/_{2}$") inside the marked outline.

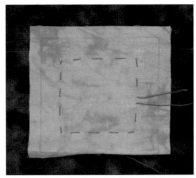

3. Bring the thread through the background fabric to the front on the marked outline. Turn under the seam allowance for approximately 12mm ($^{1}/_{2}$") and hold in place.

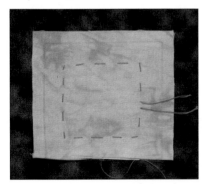

4. Stitch this section of the shape to the background fabric using slip stitch.

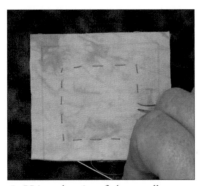

5. Using the tip of the needle, turn under the next 12mm ($^{1}/_{2}$") of the seam allowance.

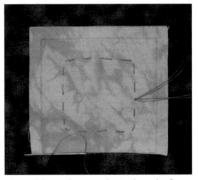

6. Hold in place and stitch as before.

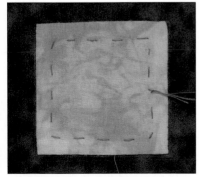

7. Continue around the entire shape in the same manner, clipping the seam allowance for any inner curves and corners as you come to them.

8. To finish, end off the thread on the back of the fabric behind the shape. Remove the pins or tacking.

QUILTING FACTS

■ It was not until about 1845 that templates became a patchwork tool. Paper was an expensive item so shapes were made by simply folding the fabric and cutting along the grain. The practice of using paper templates was far more common in England than in America.

Machine appliqué Satin stitch

1. Cut out the shape to its exact size and fuse it to the right side of the background fabric (see page 38).

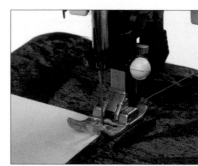

2. Set a stitch length just above 0 and a stitch width that holds the fabric securely. Position the fabrics and secure the threads.

3. Stitch along the edge of the shape, allowing the needle to enter the shape on the left and just clear it by a thread or two on the right.

4. To turn an outside corner, stitch to the end of the side. Stop with the needle down on the right hand side. Lift the presser foot. Turn fabric so next side is ready to stitch.

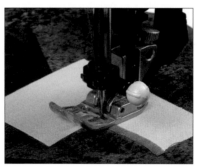

5. To turn an inside corner, stitch to the exact corner. Stop with the needle down on the left hand side. Lift presser foot. Turn the fabric so the adjacent side is in line to be stitched.

6. When stitching curves, stop with the needle down on the outside of the curve. Lift the presser foot and realign the fabric. The tighter the curve, the more frequently you will need to stop.

Zigzag stitch

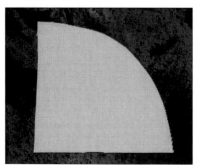

1. Cut out the shape to its exact size and fuse it to the right side of the background fabric (see page 38).

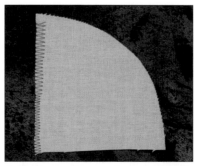

2. Set the machine to the desired stitch length and width that holds the fabric securely and compliments your design. A long wide zigzag will stand out more than a short narrow zigzag.

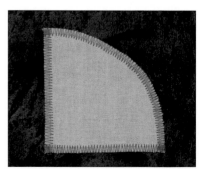

3. Position the fabrics and secure the threads. Stitch in the same manner as for machine satin stitch.

Topstitch

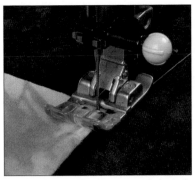

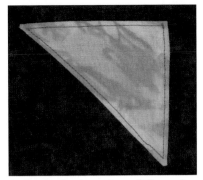

1. Cut out the shape, leaving a small seam allowance. Prepare and apply it to the right side of the background fabric using your chosen method (see pages 39 - 41). Ensure the seam allowance is turned under.

2. Set the machine to straight stitch with a stitch length of approximately 2mm (1/16"). Position the fabrics so the stitching will begin approximately 1.5mm (1/16") from the folded edge of the shape. Secure the threads.

3. Stitch slowly and carefully, maintaining an even distance from the folded edges.

Bias tubes

Bias tubes can be used to represent the stems of foliage and flowers, the lead cames of stained glass windows, Celtic knots or whatever takes your fancy. Tubes can be made in any width you choose, but it is easier to make sharp curves with a narrow tube rather than a wide one.

Making a tube with the seam allowance on the outside

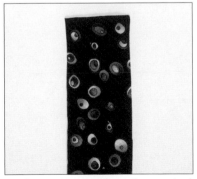

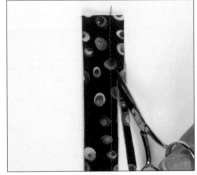

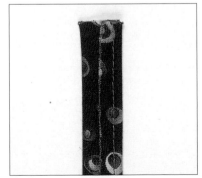

1. Cut a strip of fabric the required length plus 12mm (1/2") on the bias grain of the fabric. To determine the width of the strip, double the width of the finished tube and add 12mm (1/2").

2. With wrong sides together, fold the strip in half along the length. Stitch 6mm (1/4") from the long raw edge. Trim the seam allowance to 3mm (1/8").

3. Press with the seam allowance towards the centre and the seam offset.

Making a tube with the seam allowance on the inside

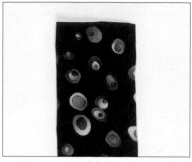

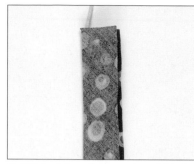

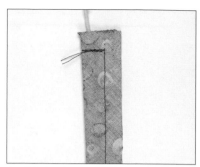

1. Cut a strip of fabric the required length plus 25mm (1") on the bias grain. To determine the width of the strip, double the width of the finished tube and add 12mm (1/2").

2. With right sides together, fold the strip in half along the length. To make turning easier, place a length of cord, which extends at each end, between the two layers.

3. Stitch 6mm (1/4") from the raw edge across one end and along the long side.

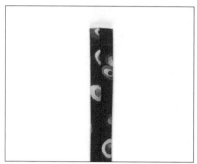

4. Trim the seam allowance if desired. Pull the free end of the cord and ease the tube back over itself, turning it to the right side.

5. Trim away the stitched end and remove the cord.

6. Press with the seam allowance at the centre or along one edge.

Making a double fold tube

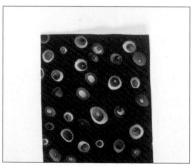

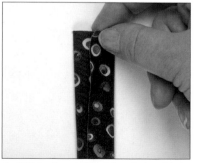

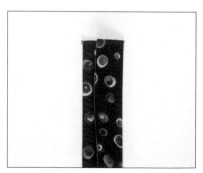

1. Cut a strip of fabric the required length plus 12mm (1/2") on the bias grain of the fabric. To determine the width of the strip, multiply the finished width by three.

2. With the right side of the fabric outermost, fold the strip into thirds, making the last section slightly narrower to hide the raw edge.

3. Press.

Appliquéing the tube

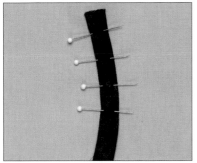

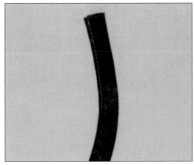

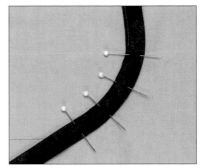

1. Mark a centre line for the tube on the right side of the background fabric. Beginning at one end and leaving 6mm (1/4") of the tube extending, pin or baste the middle of the tube along the marked line for approximately 10cm (4").

2. Machine or hand stitch one side of the tube to the fabric for the section that has been pinned or basted.

3. Pin or baste the next 10cm (4") of tube in position.

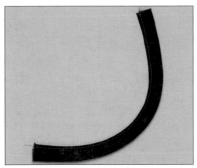

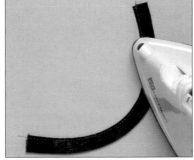

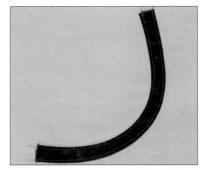

4. Continue stitching and pinning or basting until the entire tube is attached along one side.

5. Press, easing any fullness, and ensuring the tube lies flat.

6. Stitch along the remaining side of the tube in the same manner. Remove any basting.

Broderie perse

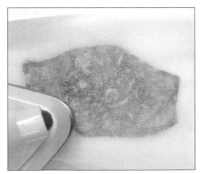

1. Roughly cut out your selected design elements from printed fabric.

2. Apply paper-backed fusible web to the wrong side of the cut-outs.

3. Carefully cut out the design to the exact size.

Broderie perse was first developed in England during the nineteenth century. It utilizes the motifs in printed fabrics to create the appliqué designs.

Broderie perse *continued*

4. Position the cut-out on the background fabric and press to fuse the two pieces together.

5. Stitch around the cut-out, either by hand or machine, using your chosen appliqué method.

QUILTING FACTS

■ Quilted petticoats were commonly worn by Dutch ladies during the eighteenth century. Because the men at the time also preferred stout women, many would wear between four and nine quilted petticoats at any one time.

Shadow appliqué

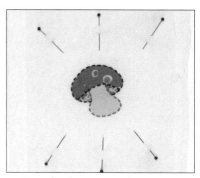

1. Cut out and apply the appliqué shapes to the right side of the background fabric using the paper-backed fusible web method on page 38.

2. Cut a piece of sheer fabric, slightly larger than the background fabric. Use fabrics such as chiffon, tulle, organza or voile. Place it over the background fabric.

3. Pin the layers together. Using a machine straight stitch or hand running stitch, stitch around the design shapes and add any internal markings.

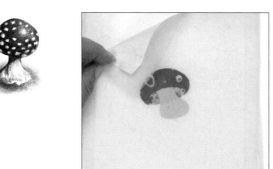

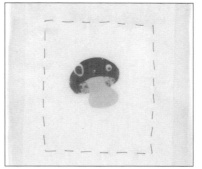

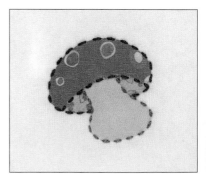

4. Alternatively, before stitching around the design, place the fabric on top of the quilt's batting and lining.

5. Baste the four layers together (see pages 91 - 92).

6. Quilt, by either hand or machine, stitching around the outer edge of the appliqué shapes.

Reverse appliqué

1. Cut two pieces of contrasting fabric the same size. Transfer the main shape to the right side of the top layer of fabric.

2. With right sides uppermost, tack the two pieces of fabric together along two adjacent sides.

3. Pin the two layers together, both inside and outside of the marked cutting line.

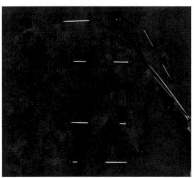

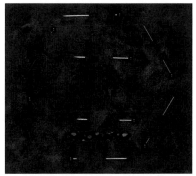

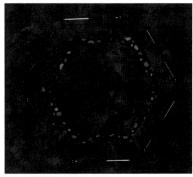

4. Cutting through the top layer of fabric only, carefully cut along the marked line.

5. Using the needle-turn appliqué technique on page 45, begin turning under the seam allowance of the inside shape and stitch to the second layer of fabric.

6. Continue around the entire shape in the same manner, clipping and folding curves and corners as required.

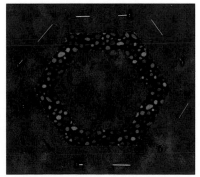

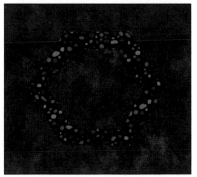

7. Stitch the remaining edge to the second layer of fabric in the same manner.

8. Remove the pins and press.

QUILTING FACTS

■ Traditionally, carded wool or pieces of woven wool were used for wadding in America. As the cotton industry developed, cotton batting became the preferred option.

Cathedral window

This special effect incorporates both piecing and fabric manipulation.

1. Piecing by hand. Cut a square of fabric. Turn under 6mm (¹/₄") of fabric along each edge. Pin, press and tack in place.

2. To find the centre, fold the square in half wrong sides together. Press.

3. Unfold and fold in half in the opposite direction. Press.

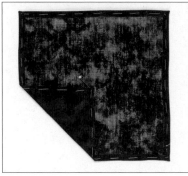

4. Unfold. With wrong sides together, fold in one corner to meet the centre. Pin and press.

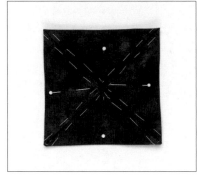

5. Fold the three remaining corners into the centre in the same manner. Pin and press.

6. With the folded side of the fabric uppermost, again fold a corner into the centre. Pin and press.

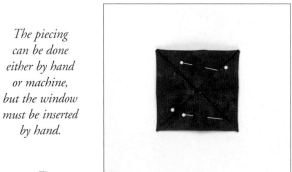

7. Fold the three remaining corners into the centre in the same manner. Pin and press.

8. At the centre, stitch the four points together, taking the stitches through all layers.

The piecing can be done either by hand or machine, but the window must be inserted by hand.

QUILTING FACTS

■ Hawaiians have developed a very distinctive style of quilt which incorporates appliqué. Originally introduced to the islands by New England missionaries in 1820, the Hawaiians developed symmetrical 'paper cut' style patterns inspired by their native flora and fauna.

Cathedral window *continued*

1. Piecing by machine. Cut a square of fabric. With right sides together, fold in half and press.

2. Using a 6mm ($1/4$") seam allowance, machine stitch along each short side.

3. Clip the corners at the fold to reduce bulk.

4. Press the seams open. At the open side and with right sides together, bring the two seams together ensuring they are aligned. Pin.

5. Using a 6mm ($1/4$") seam allowance, machine stitch the raw edges together, leaving an opening near one end for turning.

6. Press the seam open. Turn through to the right side. Press flat, ensuring the seams intersect at the centre and a square is formed. Hand stitch the opening closed.

7. With the seams side uppermost, fold in one corner to meet the centre. Pin and press.

8. Fold the three remaining corners into the centre in the same manner. Pin and press.

9. At the centre, stitch the four points together, taking the stitches through all layers.

Cathedral window *continued*

1. Inserting the windows. Make the required number of windows. Our example uses four windows.

2. Place two windows right sides together. Using tiny stitches, slip stitch the two windows together along one side. Press open. Repeat for the remaining two windows.

3. Place the two pairs of windows right sides together. Slip stitch together along one long side in the same manner as before. Press open.

4. To determine the required size of each 'window', measure from one corner to the stitched centre of one pieced square. Cut four squares to this measurement from contrasting fabric for the 'windows'.

5. Place one contrasting square, over the diamond shape formed when two folded squares were pieced together. It will cover the seam between the two squares.

6. Fold one edge of the background over the edge of the 'window'.

7. Neatly hand stitch the folded edge to the window.

8. Repeat steps 6 and 7 on the three remaining sides of the 'window'.

9. Insert the required number of 'windows' in the same manner.

Ruching Grid ruching

Ruching is a decorative form of gathering fabric. The ruched pieces need to be stabilized.

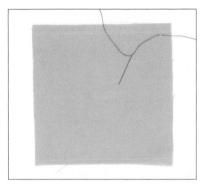

1. Cut a large square of fabric. Using thread longer than twice the width of the fabric square, take it through the fabric on the right hand side near the top. Leave a tail of thread extending.

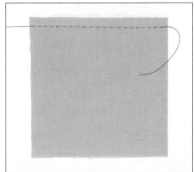

2. Work a row of running stitch across the top of the fabric.

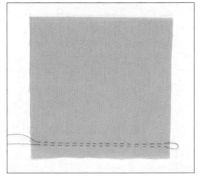

3. Turn the fabric and work running stitch back across the fabric just above the first row. Cut the thread leaving a tail extending.

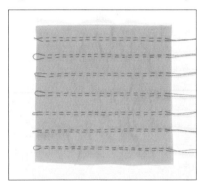

4. Continue working pairs of rows across the fabric in the same manner until it is completely covered.

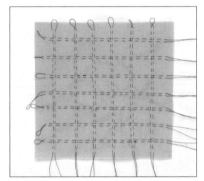

5. Work pairs of running stitch rows in the same manner, but at right angles to the previous rows.

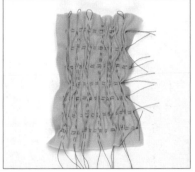

6. Carefully pull the threads on one side to gather the fabric. Tie off the threads.

7. Carefully pull up the threads on the adjacent side in the same manner. Tie off the threads.

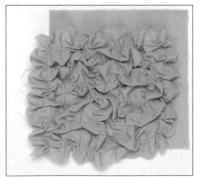

8. To stabilize the ruching, cut a piece of fabric the same size as the finished ruched piece.

9. With right sides uppermost, place the ruched fabric on the flat fabric. Hand stitch around all sides.

Ruching can bring added texture and dimension to a quilt top.

Circular ruching

1. Trace the template on page 128 and transfer the markings to the right side of the fabric. (Note: enlarge or reduce the template using a photocopier.)

2. Cut the fabric along the outer line of dots to form a circle.

3. Fold under the edge of the fabric between two outer dots (A and C).

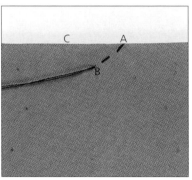

4. Bring a knotted and doubled thread through the folded edge at A. Work running stitch to the inner dot between A and C (B).

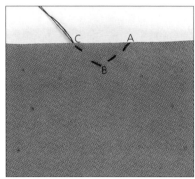

5. Work running stitch from B to C, forming a zigzag.

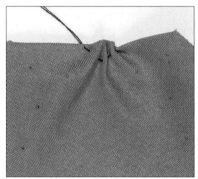

6. Pull up the running stitches to gather the fabric.

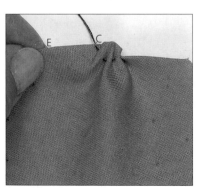

7. Fold under the fabric between C and the next outer dot (E).

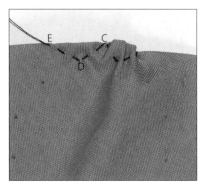

8. Work running stitch to the next inner dot (D), and then to E to form a second zigzag.

9. Pull up the running stitches to gather this section of fabric.

Circular ruching *continued*

10. Continue folding, stitching and gathering, one section at a time, until reaching the beginning.

11. Secure the thread on the back of the ruched fabric.

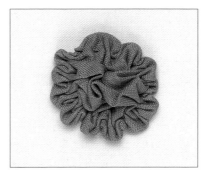

12. Position the ruched fabric onto a piece of flat fabric.

13. Attach the ruched fabric to the flat fabric by working a stab stitch in each indent of the ruched fabric's edge.

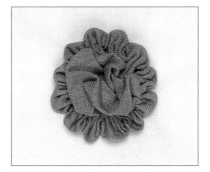

14. Arrange the puffiness in the middle until you achieve the desired appearance.

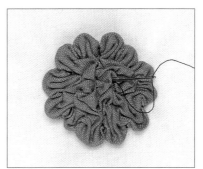

15. Secure the folds with tiny, randomly placed stab stitches.

Prairie points (or shark's teeth)
Individual prairie points - method one

1. Cut a square of fabric with sides two times plus 12mm (¹/2") longer than the size of the required 'point'. Press.

2. Fold the fabric in half diagonally to form a triangle. Press.

3. Fold in half again, ensuring all edges are even. Press. It is now ready to be attached to the quilt top.

These pointed shapes can be inserted into a seam to create a three-dimensional effect, or used around the edge of the quilt top. The edge along which all raw edges of fabric fall is inserted into the seam.

Individual prairie points - method two

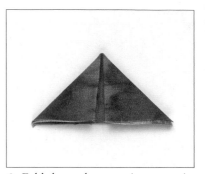

1. Cut a square of fabric with sides two times plus 12mm ($^1/_2$") longer than the size of the required 'point'. Fold in half to form a rectangle. Press.

2. With the folded edge of the rectangle at the top, fold down one corner so the raw edges meet at the lower edge. Press.

3. Fold down the opposite corner in the same manner. Press. It is now ready to be attached to the quilt top.

Multiple prairie points

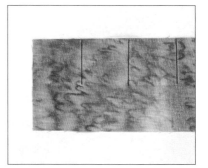

1. Determine the size of the squares needed following the instructions in step 1 above. Cut a strip of fabric that is twice the width of this measurement.

2. Fold the strip in half along the length and press.

3. Open out. Beginning at one end, mark the strip at evenly spaced intervals, using the measurement worked out at step 1. Rule a line at each mark from the fabric's edge to the foldline.

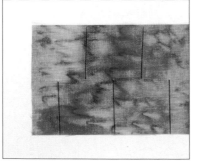

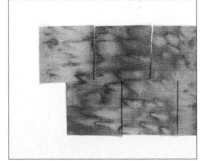

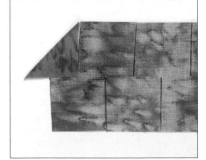

4. Beginning halfway along the first marked square, mark the second half of the strip in the same manner.

5. Cut along each marked line from the edge to the foldline. Cut away the partial squares at each end.

6. Fold the first square in half to form a triangle, folding the outermost corner, towards the corner of the adjacent square at the foldline. Press.

Multiple prairie points *continued*

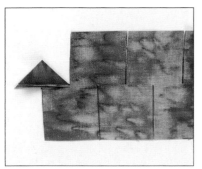

7. Fold in half again so all raw edges are along the foldline. Press.

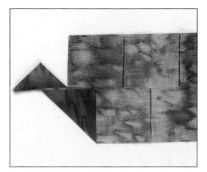

8. Fold the first square, on the opposite side of the foldline, in half to form a triangle. Press.

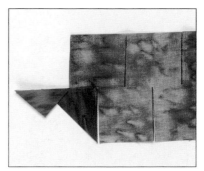

9. Fold down the first triangle so it lies across the triangle just formed.

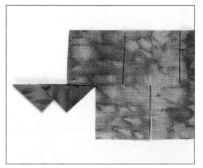

10. Fold the second triangle in half so it partially covers the first triangle. All the raw edges are along the foldline.

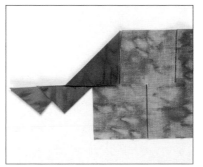

11. Fold the third square of fabric in half following step 6. Press.

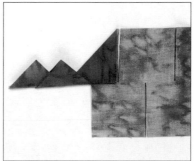

12. Fold the first two 'points' up so they partially cover the third triangle.

13. Fold the third triangle in half, partially enclosing the second 'point'. Press.

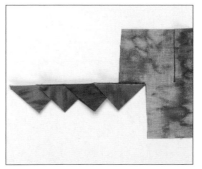

14. Using the next square of fabric on the opposite side, work the fourth 'point' in the same manner.

15. Continue in the same manner until all points are made.

Slashing and chenilling Slashing

Using fabrics of different colours and textures adds further interest to the effects that can be achieved.

1. With right sides uppermost, place approximately five pieces of fabric together, one on top of the other.

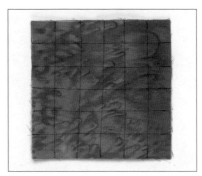

2. Machine stitch the pieces together, using a grid pattern. Keeping the lines of stitching approx 2.5cm (1") apart, works well for this technique.

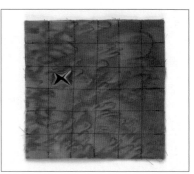

3. Using small, sharp scissors, snip diagonally through some, or all except the last layer of fabric, within one stitched square.

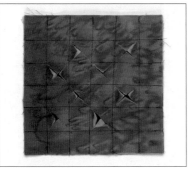

4. Repeat the procedure in the desired squares.

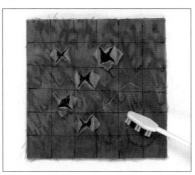

5. Brush the fabric with a stiff brush to help separate the cut edges and fray the fabric. Alternatively, wash and tumble dry.

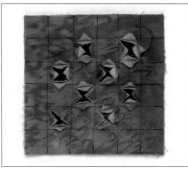

6. **Completed slashing.**

Chenilling

Several layers of fabric are stitched together and then cut on the bias. The last layer is not cut at all.

1. Layer the fabric as in step 1 above. Machine stitch diagonally through all layers, placing the rows approx 12 - 20mm (1/2 - 3/4") apart.

2. Using small, sharp scissors, snip between the lines of stitching through all except the last layer of fabric.

3. Brush the fabric with a stiff brush to help separate the cut edges and fray the fabric. Alternatively, wash and tumble dry.

Tucking

Tucks can be used to add texture to an entire quilt top or to individual blocks. By varying the spacing, depth and folding of tucks a wide variety of effects can be achieved.

Spaced tucks

1. Cut a rectangle of fabric. Rule lines at regular intervals to mark the folded edges of the tucks.

2. With wrong sides together, fold the fabric along the first marked line.

3. Stitch through both layers of fabric at the desired distance from the folded edge. Press.

4. Unfold the fabric. With wrong sides together, refold the fabric along the second marked line.

5. Stitch in the same manner as before. Unfold the fabric. Press.

6. Continue working tucks, following steps 2 and 3, to the end of the fabric. Remove all markings. Press each tuck to one side.

HINTS ON TUCKS

■ Tucking 'shrinks' the size of your fabric so always begin with a piece much larger than your requirements for the finished piece. Alternatively, add extensions to the tucked fabric once the tucking is finished.

■ For all but centred tucks, press a tuck in the wrong direction first and then press it in the right direction, using a pressing cloth to protect the fabric. Finally, press it from the wrong side of the fabric.

■ Tucks are easier to stitch on the straight grain of the fabric. Those worked on the bias will not hold a sharp edge.

■ To aid construction, secure the ends of tucks by basting within the seam allowance.

■ When stitching across tucks (such as bubble tucks and undulated tucks), the wider the tucks, the wider the space between the rows of cross stitching needs to be.

Blind, graduated and centred tucks

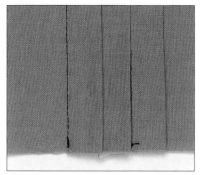

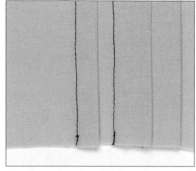

Blind tucks. Work as for spaced tucks but ensure the space between each tuck is equal to or less than the width of the tuck.

Graduated tucks. Work as for spaced tucks but the spaces between the tucks and the width of each tuck can vary.

Centred tucks. Work as for spaced tucks but press each tuck so the centre of the tuck aligns with the seam.

Undulated tucks

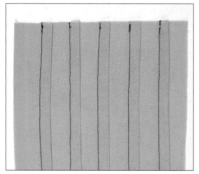

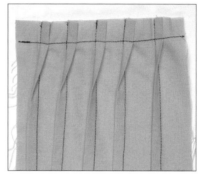

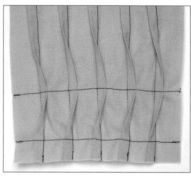

1. Begin by working either spaced, blind or graduated tucks following the previous instructions.

2. Topstitch across the fabric at right angles to the tucks.

3. Turn the fabric around. Beginning from the opposite side to the first row, stitch a second row of topstitching.

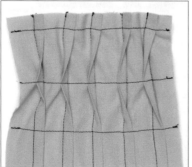

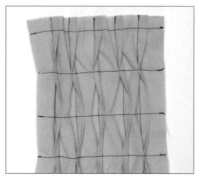

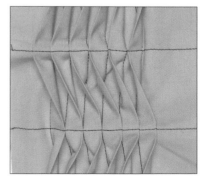

4. Work a third row, stitching in the same direction as the first row.

5. Continue in the same manner, always alternating the direction of the topstitching from row to row, until reaching the end of the fabric.

6. Undulated tucks using blind tucks as the foundation.

Leave enough space between each row of topstitching for the pleats to reverse direction. If they are too close together, the pleats will drag up the fabric.

Bubble tucks

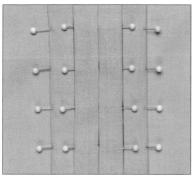

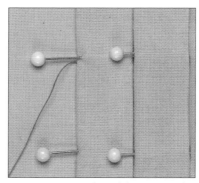

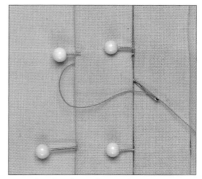

1. Begin by working centred tucks following the previous instructions. Mark each tuck with evenly spaced pins to indicate stitching positions.

2. Using strong thread, bring it to the front at the seam, behind the left hand side of the tuck.

3. Take the thread over the tuck to the other side. Take the needle to the back of the fabric on the seam behind the right hand side of the tuck.

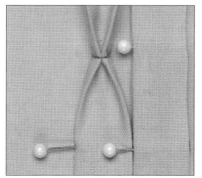

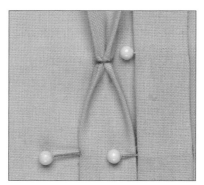

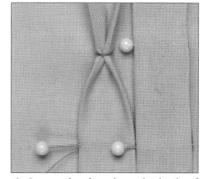

4. Pull the thread firmly, crushing the fabric at this point.

5. Repeat steps 2 - 4 one more time.

6. Secure the thread on the back of the fabric and trim. Alternatively, carry the thread to the next marked position on the tuck. Bring it to the front at the seam, behind the left hand side of the tuck.

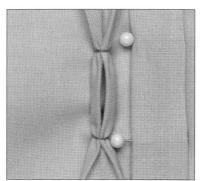

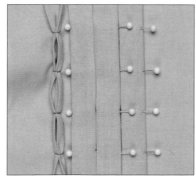

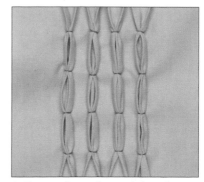

7. Work two stitches in the same manner as before, pulling each stitch firmly to crush the pleat.

8. Continue to the end of the pleat in the same manner.

9. Repeat for each remaining pleat.

Suffolk puffs

Suffolk puffs are made from a circle of fabric that is hand gathered around the outer edge.

....

64

1. Using a circular template of the required size, cut out a circle of fabric. Thread a needle with matching machine sewing thread.

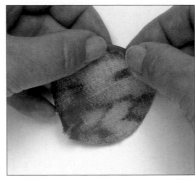

2. With wrong sides together, fold under 3mm ($^1/_8$") around the entire edge of the circle and finger press.

3. Beginning on the wrong side and using running stitches, stitch along the folded edge.

4. Firmly pull up the running stitches to gather the fabric.

5. Secure the thread with 2 - 3 tiny back stitches. Take the thread inside the puff and re-emerge a short distance away.

6. Flatten the puff, keeping the gathering at the centre. Gently pull the thread and snip it close to the fabric.

The longer the running stitches used for the gathering, the smaller the opening at the centre will be. Conversely, using tiny running stitches will result in a larger opening at the centre.

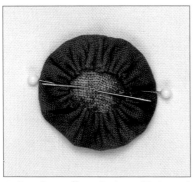

7. Lay the puff on the base fabric and pin in position.

8. Secure the puff to the quilt top with surface embroidery, such as French and colonial knots, or slip stitched around the outer edge.

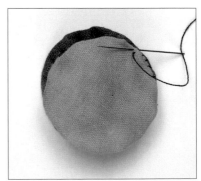

9. Alternatively, place two puffs, right sides together. Take 3 - 4 stitches close together through the folded edges of both puffs.

Suffolk puffs *continued*

10. End off the thread and open out the puffs.

11. Multiple Suffolk puffs can be joined together in this manner.

12. As a variation, slip a small circle of fabric inside the puff before pulling up the gathering thread.

Yo-yos

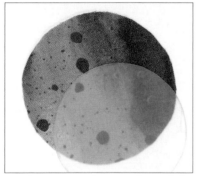

1. Using a circular template of the required size, cut out a circle of fabric. Thread a needle with matching machine sewing thread.

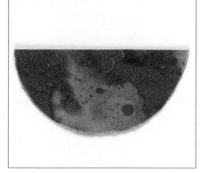

2. With wrong sides together, fold the circle in half and press.

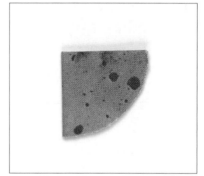

3. Fold the fabric in half again and press.

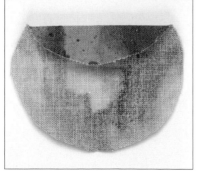

4. Unfold. With wrong sides together, fold one side so the foldline is aligned and the outer edge meets the centre point. Finger press.

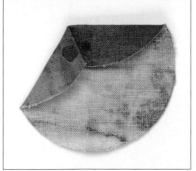

5. Fold the adjacent side of the fabric so the end of the previous fold meets the centre. Finger press.

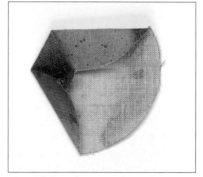

6. Fold the adjacent side to the centre in the same manner as step 5.

....

65

Each yo-yo is created from a circle of fabric, which is carefully folded and then attached to the quilt top at the centre.

Yo-yos *continued*

7. Repeat the procedure two more times.

8. Fold over the remaining section of fabric so the point finishes at the centre.

9. Using the needle and thread, secure the points at the centre.

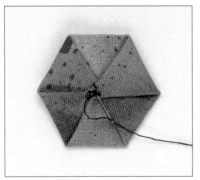

10. Using the same thread, attach the centre of the yo-yo to the quilt top.

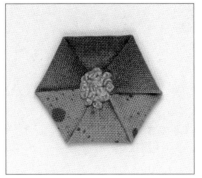

11. Cover the centre with tightly clustered French or colonial knots.

12. Alternatively, cover the centre with a button.

SUFFOLK PUFFS AND YO-YOS

■ To determine the size of the circle you need to use for a Suffolk puff, multiply the diameter of the desired puff by two and add 12mm ($^1/_2$").

■ The centre of a yo-yo can be filled with all sorts of pretty and interesting objects such as beads,

buttons, charms and trinkets. Just ensure that all the layers of fabric are securely held in place.

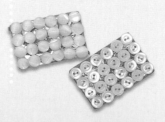

Embroidery

Embellishing with surface embroidery is an integral part of crazy patchwork, but it can be used to decorate any quilt. There are too many different embroidery stitches and combinations of stitches to include them all here. The stitches featured are those most commonly used for crazy patchwork.

Blanket stitch

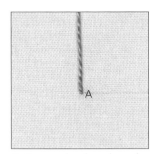

1. Secure the thread on the back of the fabric and bring it to the front at A.

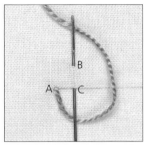

2. Take the needle to the back at B and re-emerge at C. Ensure the thread is under the tip of the needle.

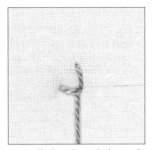

3. Pull the thread through until it lies snugly against the emerging thread but does not distort the fabric.

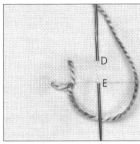

4. Take the needle to the back at D and re-emerge at E. Ensure the thread lies under the tip of the needle.

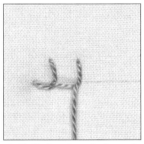

5. Pull the thread through as before.

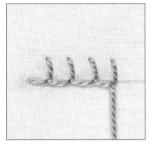

6. Continue working blanket stitches in the same manner.

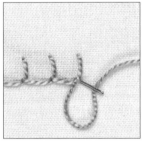

7. To finish, take the needle to the back of the fabric just over the last loop.

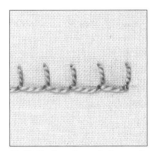

8. Pull the thread through and end off on the back of the fabric.

EMBROIDERY THREADS AND NEEDLES

■ Generally use lengths of embroidery thread approximately 50cm (20") long. However, when using metallic or rayon threads, use shorter lengths as these threads can be difficult to manage.

■ When using stranded thread, always 'strip' the thread to give better coverage. This entails separating all the strands and then putting back together the number you wish to use.

■ Ensure the needle you are using has a large enough eye to protect the thread. It should make a hole in the fabric that the thread will pass through easily but not so large that the thread does not fill the hole. Crewel needles are excellent for working most embroidery stitches.

■ Create your own variegated threads by combining strands of different colours in the needle at the same time.

Blanket stitch - long and short

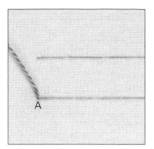

1. Secure the thread on the back of the fabric and bring it to the front at A.

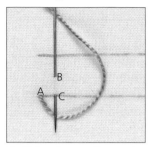

2. Take the needle to the back at B and re-emerge at C. Ensure the thread is under the tip of the needle.

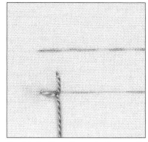

3. Pull the thread through until it lies snugly against the emerging thread but does not distort the fabric.

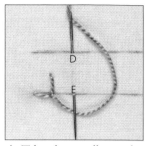

4. Take the needle to the back at D and re-emerge at E. This is parallel to the previous stitch but longer. Ensure the thread lies under the tip of the needle.

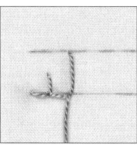

5. Pull the thread through as before.

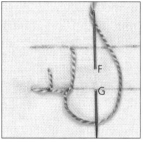

6. Take the needle to the back at F and re-emerge at G to make a stitch the same length as the first stitch. Ensure the thread lies under the tip of the needle.

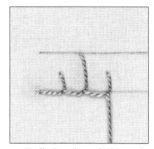

7. Pull the thread through as before.

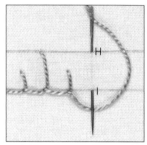

8. Take the needle to the back at H and re-emerge at I to make a stitch the same length as the second stitch. Ensure the thread lies under the tip of the needle.

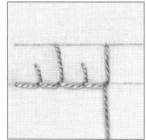

9. Pull the thread through as before.

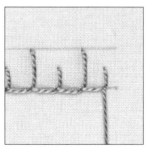

10. Continue working stitches in the same manner.

11. To finish, take the needle to the back of the fabric just over the last loop.

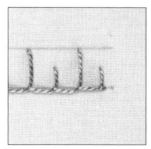

12. Pull the thread through and end off on the back of the fabric.

....

68

If your thread untwists or overtwists while stitching, let the needle dangle freely. The thread will spin back to the correct amount of twist.

Chain stitch

1. Secure the thread on the back of the fabric and bring it to the front at A.

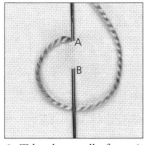

2. Take the needle from A to B, using the same hole in the fabric at A. Loop the thread under the tip of the needle.

3. Pull the thread through until the loop lies snugly against the emerging thread.

4. Take the needle through the same hole in the fabric at B and re-emerge at C. Loop the thread under the tip of the needle.

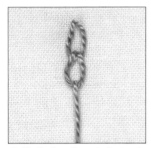

5. Pull the thread through as before.

6. Continue working stitches in the same manner.

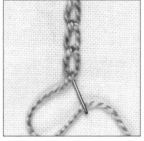

7. To finish, take the needle to the back just over the last loop.

8. Pull the thread through and end off on the back of the fabric.

Detached chain (or lazy daisy stitch)

1. Secure the thread on the back of the fabric and bring it to the front at A. This is the base of the stitch.

2. Hold the thread to the left.

3. Take the needle to the back at A, through the same hole in the fabric. Re-emerge at B. Loop the thread under the tip of the needle.

4. Pull the thread through. The tighter you pull, the thinner the stitch will become.

Detached chain *continued*

5. To finish, take the needle to the back just over the end of the loop.

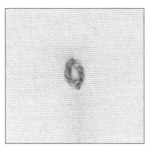

6. Pull the thread through and end off on the back of the fabric.

EMBROIDERY STITCHES

■ Detached chains and chain stitches will become 'skinny' if the thread is pulled too firmly. For 'plump' stitches, pull the thread through the fabric smoothly and slowly.
■ To prevent the stitches from puckering the fabric, work with the fabric in an embroidery hoop. Use an up and down 'stabbing' motion to work the stitches rather than scooping the needle through the fabric.

Feather stitch

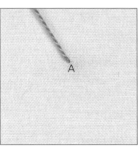

1. Bring the needle to the front at A. This will be the left hand side of the stitch.

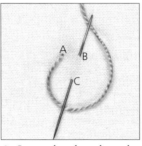

2. Loop the thread to the right and take the needle from B to C. Ensure the thread is under the tip of the needle.

3. Pull the thread through in a downward movement and hold firmly with your thumb.

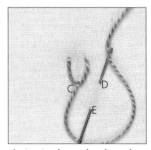

4. Again, loop the thread to the right and take the needle from D to E. Ensure the thread is under the tip of the needle.

5. Pull the thread through in the same manner as before.

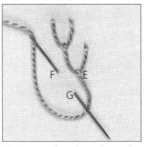

6. Loop the thread to the left and take the needle from F to G. Ensure the thread is under the tip of the needle.

7. Pull the thread through. Continue working stitches in the same manner.

8. To finish, take the needle to the back of the fabric just over the last loop. Pull the thread through and end off.

Fly stitch

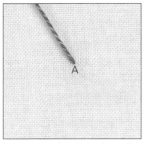 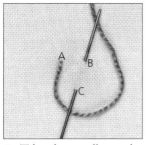 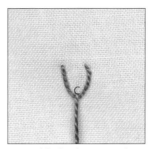 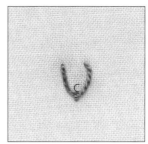

1. Secure the thread on the back of the fabric and bring it to the front at A. This will be the left hand side of the stitch.

2. Take the needle to the back at B and re-emerge at C. Loop the thread under the tip of the needle.

3. Hold the loop in place with your thumb (thumb not shown). Pull the thread until the loop lies snugly against C.

4. Take the thread to the back of the fabric below C to anchor the loop. End off the thread on the back of the fabric.

French knot

   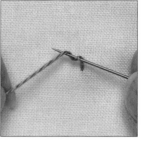

1. Secure the thread on the back of the fabric and bring it to the front at the position for the knot.

2. Hold the thread firmly approximately 3cm (1 1/8") from the fabric.

3. Take the thread over the needle, ensuring the needle points away from the fabric.

4. Wrap the thread around the needle. Keeping the thread taut, turn the tip of the needle towards the fabric.

   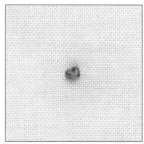

5. Take the tip of the needle to the back of the fabric approximately 1 - 2 fabric threads away from where it emerged.

6. Slide the knot down the needle onto the fabric. Pull the thread until the knot is firmly around the needle.

7. Push the needle through the fabric. Hold the knot in place with your thumb and pull the thread through (thumb not shown).

8. Pull until the loop of thread completely disappears. End off on the back of the fabric.

Herringbone stitch

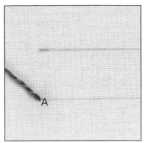

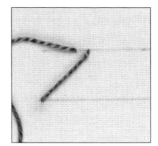

1. Mark two stitching guidelines on the right side of the fabric. Bring the thread to the front at A, on the left hand side of the lower line.

2. With the thread below the needle, take the needle from right to left on the upper line as shown.

3. Pull the thread through.

4. With the thread above the needle, take the needle from right to left on the lower line.

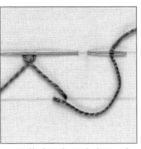

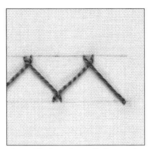

5. Pull the thread through. With the thread below the needle, take the needle from right to left on the upper line.

6. Pull the thread through. Continue working stitches in the same manner, alternating between the upper and lower lines. End off on the back of the fabric.

QUILTING FACTS

■ Log cabin patchwork is also known as Canadian patchwork. It is believed that the settlers who moved to the Northern Territories after the American Revolution were the originators of this style of patchwork. The pattern represents a cabin roof with its strong central chimney.

Pistil stitch

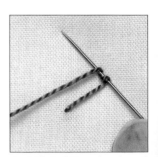

1. Secure the thread on the back of the fabric and bring it to the front at A, the base of the stitch.

2. Holding the thread firmly in the left hand, wrap the thread over the needle.

3. Keeping the thread taut, wrap it around the needle in an anti-clockwise direction for the required number of wraps.

4. Still holding the thread taut, turn the needle towards the fabric.

Pistil stitch *continued*

5. Push the tip of the needle through the fabric at the required position.

6. Keeping tension on the thread, slide the wraps down the needle onto the fabric.

7. Keeping your thumb over the wraps, begin to pull the thread through (thumb not shown).

8. Pull the thread all the way through and end off on the back of the fabric.

Stem stitch

1. Draw a line on the fabric. Secure the thread on the back of the fabric and bring it to the front at A, on the left hand end.

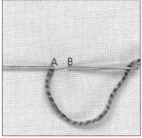

2. With the thread below the needle, take the needle to the back at B and re-emerge at A.

3. Pull the thread through to complete the first stitch.

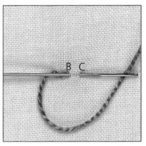

4. Again with the thread below the needle, take the needle to the back at C and re-emerge at B.

5. Pull the thread through to complete the second stitch.

6. Continue working stitches in the same manner, always keeping the thread below the needle.

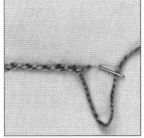

7. To finish, take the needle to the back for the last stitch. Do not re-emerge.

8. Pull the thread through and end off on the back of the fabric.

Couching

Couching is a particularly useful technique. It allows you to attach all sorts of treasures and decorative pieces to your quilt top. Ribbons, braids, cords and ornamental threads can all be secured using the method below.

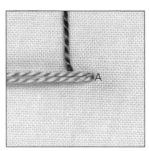

1. Secure the foundation thread on the back of the fabric and bring it to the front at A. Lay it on the fabric.

2. Secure the couching thread on the back of the fabric and bring it to the front just above the laid thread near A.

3. Take the needle over the laid thread and to the back of the fabric.

4. Pull the thread through to form the first couching stitch.

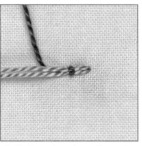   

5. Bring the thread to the front just above the laid thread and a short distance away from the first couching stitch.

6. Pull the thread through. Continue working stitches in the same manner for the required distance.

7. Take the couching thread to the back of the fabric and end off.

8. Take the laid thread to the back of the fabric and end off.

COUCHING

■ Couching stitches should hold the laid thread firmly but not squeeze it.

■ Almost any surface embroidery stitch can be used as an ornamental couching stitch.

■ Ensure both your laid threads and couching threads have care requirements that are compatible with the fabrics and intended use of the quilt.

BEADING

■ Always use a slender needle with a small eye that will easily pass through the holes in the beads. Forcing a needle through a too small hole can result in the bead cracking.

■ Use a special beading thread, such a Nymo, for attaching beads. Alternatively, use machine sewing thread and pass it through some beeswax to add strength.

Beading Attaching a bead

method one

1. Secure the thread on the back of the fabric and bring it to the front. Thread the bead onto the needle.

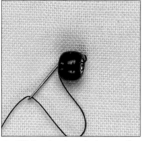

2. Slide the bead down the thread to the fabric. Take the needle to the back at the end of the bead.

3. Pull the thread through. Re-emerge at the other end of the bead.

4. Take the needle through the bead again.

5. Pull the thread through. Take the needle to the back of the fabric at the end of the bead.

6. Pull the thread through. End off on the back of the fabric.

method two

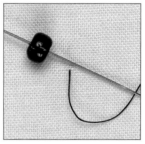

1. Secure the thread on the back of the fabric and bring it to the front. Thread the bead onto the needle.

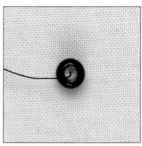

2. Slide the bead down the thread to the fabric. Hold the bead on the fabric so the hole is uppermost.

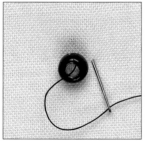

3. Take the needle to the back of the fabric on one side of the bead.

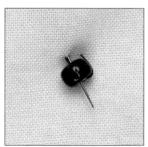

4. Pull the thread through. Bring the needle up through the bead again.

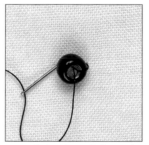

5. Pull the thread through. Take the needle to the back of the fabric on the other side of the bead.

6. Pull the thread through. End off on the back of the fabric.

Attaching a string of beads

method one

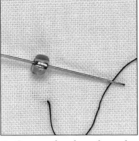

1. Secure the thread on the back of the fabric and bring it to the front. Thread a bead onto the needle.

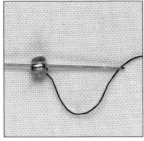

2. Attach the bead following steps 2 - 4 of method 1 on page 75.

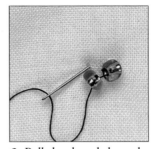

3. Pull the thread through. Thread a second bead onto the needle. Take the needle to the back of the fabric at the end of the bead.

4. Pull the thread through. Re-emerge between the two beads.

5. Take the needle through the second bead again.

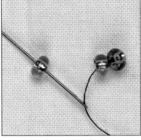

6. Pull the thread through. Thread a third bead onto the needle.

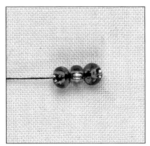

7. Secure the bead to the fabric in the same manner as before.

8. Continue attaching the required number of beads in the same manner. After attaching the last bead, take the thread to the back of the fabric and secure.

method two

1. Secure the thread on the back of the fabric and bring it to the front. Thread the required number of beads onto the needle.

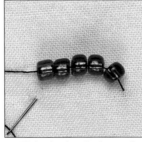

2. Slide the beads down the thread. Take the needle to the back of the fabric at the required position.

3. Pull the thread through. Bring the needle to the front between the last two beads.

4. Pull the thread through. Take the needle to the back of the fabric just over the thread between the last two beads.

Attaching a string of beads - method two *continued*

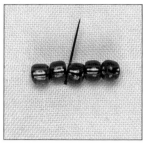

5. Pull the thread through. Re-emerge between the next two beads.

6. Pull the thread through. Take it to the back of the fabric just over the thread between the two beads.

7. Pull the thread through. Continue couching the thread between the beads in the same manner.

8. To finish, secure the thread on the back of the fabric after the last couching stitch.

Attaching a circle of beads

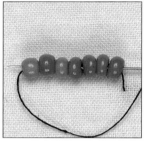

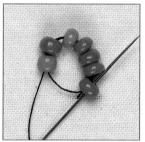

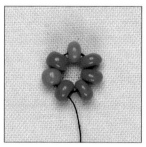

1. Secure the thread on the back of the fabric and bring it to the front. Thread the required number of beads onto the needle.

2. Pull the thread through. Take the needle through all beads in the same order that they were first threaded onto the needle.

3. Pull the thread through. Take the needle through the first bead.

4. Pull the thread firmly to pull the beads into a circle.

5. Position the circle on the fabric. Take the needle to the back of the fabric between the first and second beads.

6. Pull the thread through. Re-emerge between the second and third beads.

7. Couch the beads to the fabric following steps 4 - 7 of method 2 on pages 76 - 77.

8. To finish, secure the thread on the back of the fabric after the last couching stitch.

....

77

Blocking

No matter how meticulous you are, it is very rare for pieced blocks to turn out flat or even identical. For best results, each block needs to be blocked before assembling the quilt top.

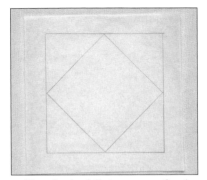

1. Transfer the full size pattern for the block to a piece of paper.

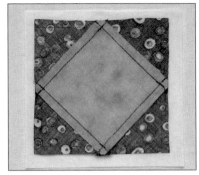

2. Place the paper pattern onto your ironing board or similar padded surface. Place the block face down over the paper pattern.

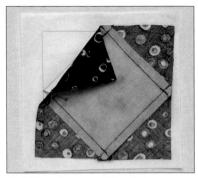

3. Using fine small headed pins (eg silk pins) and starting from the centre, take a pin through a seam or corner. Push it through the corresponding place on the paper pattern and then into the padded surface.

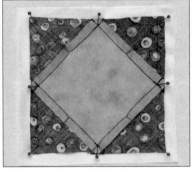

4. Continue pinning in this manner, slightly stretching or easing the block to fit the pattern.

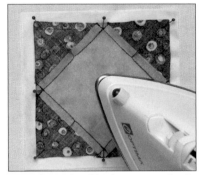

5. When the block is completely pinned out, apply steam to the entire piece by holding a steam iron just above the fabric and slowly moving it about. Do not press.

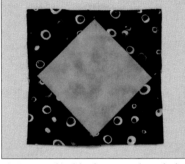

6. Leave the block to cool and dry completely. Remove the pins and handle gently until it is sewn into the quilt top.

ASSEMBLING THE QUILT TOP

■ Do not wash the quilt top until the quilt is finished as the edges may fray.

■ Before assembling the quilt top, experiment with the placement of blocks by laying them all out flat and arranging and re-arranging them to discover the most pleasing effect. If sashing and borders are to be included in the quilt top, lay these pieces out as well.

■ Blocks can be pinned to a large design board or laid out on the floor. The advantage of the design board is that you can view the pieces from a greater distance and have a better idea of the overall effect. If you have laid the blocks out on the floor, stand on a chair or step ladder to put more distance between your eyes and the laid out pieces.

Setting blocks together

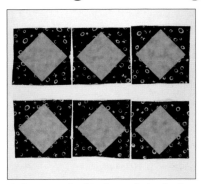

1. Lay out the blocks and check that they are correctly positioned.

2. Hand or machine stitch all the blocks in the first row together to form a strip.

3. Repeat for the remaining rows.

4. Press all the seams of the first row in the same direction.

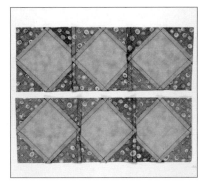

5. Press all the seams of the second row in the opposite direction to those of the first row. Repeat for the remaining rows, alternating the direction from row to row.

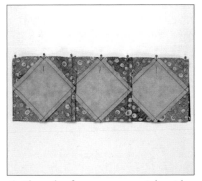

6. Place the first two rows right sides together. Pin the ends and then pin the seams together, ensuring they are accurately aligned.

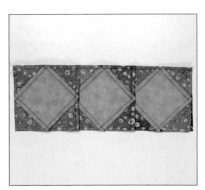

7. Hand or machine stitch the two rows together. Press.

8. With right sides together, pin the top of the third row to the lower edge of the second row in the same manner as before.

9. Stitch and press. Continue attaching the remaining rows in the same manner.

Sashing Sashing without cornerstones

Sashing creates a framework around each block. It is an alternative to setting the blocks together.

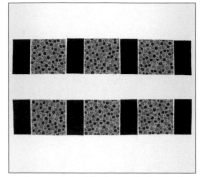

1. Lay out the blocks and check that they are correctly positioned. Cut sashing strips of fabric the same height as the blocks and place them between the blocks in each row.

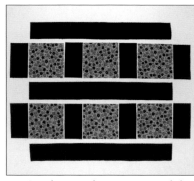

2. Cut long sashing strips and lay them between the rows.

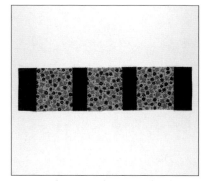

3. Hand or machine stitch all the blocks and strips in the first row together to form a long strip.

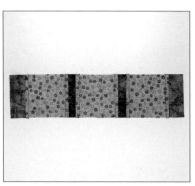

4. Press all the seam allowances towards the sashing.

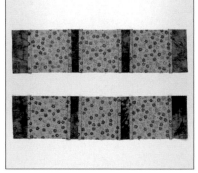

5. Stitch and press the blocks and sashing pieces for the remaining rows in the same manner.

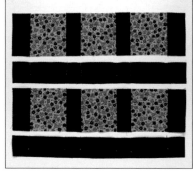

6. Mark the long sashing strips with pins at the positions that align with the block seams.

As a guide, the finished sashing should be approximately one quarter the width of the finished blocks.

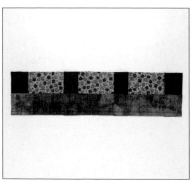

7. With right sides together and matching markings with seams, pin one long strip to a row of blocks. Stitch.

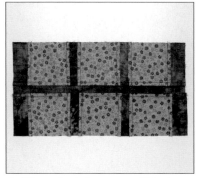

8. Pin and stitch a row of blocks to the other edge of the strip. Press the seam allowances towards the sashing.

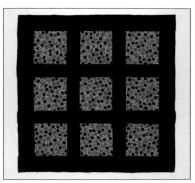

9. Continue attaching the remaining strips in the same manner.

Sashing with cornerstones

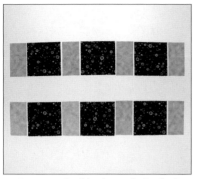

1. Lay out the blocks and check that they are correctly positioned. Cut sashing strips of fabric the same height as the blocks and place them between the blocks in each row.

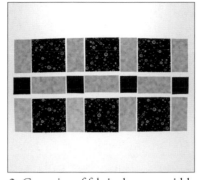

2. Cut strips of fabric the same width as the blocks and place them between the upper and lower edges of the blocks. Cut the cornerstones and position them between these strips.

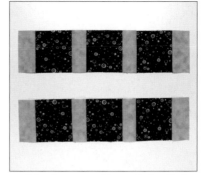

3. Hand or machine stitch all the blocks and sashing strips in the first row together to form a long strip. Repeat for the remaining rows.

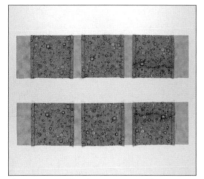

4. Press all the seam allowances towards the sashing.

5. Hand or machine stitch all the rows of cornerstones and sashing strips in the same manner.

6. With right sides together and matching markings with seamlines, pin one long strip to a row of blocks.

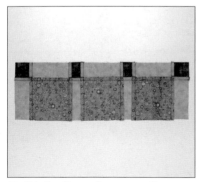

7. Stitch. Press the seam allowance towards the sashing.

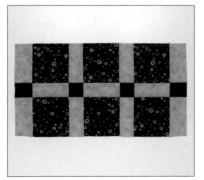

8. Pin and stitch a row of blocks to the other edge of the sashing strip. Press as before.

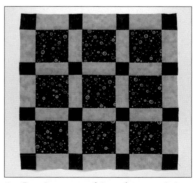

9. Continue attaching the remaining sashing strips in the same manner.

To ensure your quilt will lie flat and be a proper square or rectangle, measure border pieces accurately. Borders on opposite sides need to be the same length.

Cut side borders to measure the same length as the sides of the quilt top. Cut the upper and lower borders to measure the same as the end of the quilt top plus twice the border strip width, less 2.5cm (1").

Borders Measuring for borders

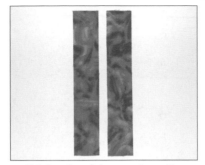

1. Side borders. Measure the quilt top along both sides and down the centre. Add the measurements together and divide by 3. Cut the side borders to this measurement plus enough to finish the ends by your chosen method.

2. Top and bottom borders. Measure the quilt top along the top and bottom and across the centre. Calculate the measurement as in step 1. Cut to this measurement plus enough to finish the ends by your chosen method.

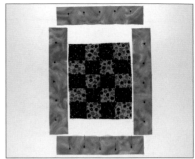

3. Place a pin at each end of one side border to mark the same measurement as the side of the quilt top (the measurement from step 1). Aligning pins, fold the border into quarters. Mark each fold with a pin. Repeat for the remaining pieces.

Butted corners

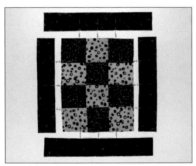

1. Mark the sides and ends of the quilt top with pins at the quarter and halfway points. Mark the border strips in the same manner (see above).

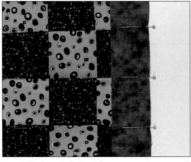

2. With right sides together and matching pins, pin one side border to one side of the quilt top. Slightly stretch or ease the border as necessary.

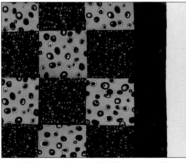

3. Using a 6mm (1/4") seam allowance, hand or machine stitch the border to the quilt top. Press the seam towards the border.

4. Attach the border to the opposite side of the quilt top in the same manner and press as before.

5. Pin and stitch the upper border following steps 2 - 3. Ensure the ends align with the outer edges of the side borders. Press as before.

6. Attach the border to the opposite end of the quilt top in the same manner and press as before.

Square corners

Cut side borders to measure the same length as the sides of the quilt top. Cut end borders to measure the same as the ends of the quilt top. Cut four corner squares the same size as the width of the border pieces.

1. Attach the side borders following steps 1 - 4 of butted corners on the previous page.

2. With right sides together, pin and stitch a corner square to each end of the upper and lower border pieces. Press the seam allowances away from the squares.

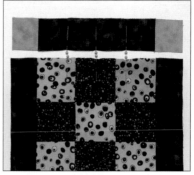

3. Mark the ends of the quilt top with pins at the quarter and halfway points. Ensure the border strips are marked in the same manner (see the previous page).

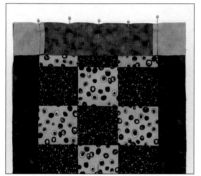

4. With right sides together and matching marks and seams, pin the upper border to the upper edge of the quilt top.

5. Stitch. Press the seam allowances towards the border.

6. Attach the remaining border piece in the same manner.

SASHING AND BORDERS

■ Plan borders at the initial design stages of your quilt. Borders added as an afterthought tend to either dominate or dilute the overall effect of the design.

■ Ensure the quilt top is well pressed and squared before measuring for the border pieces.

■ Use a metal tape measure to measure your quilt top as there is less likely to be any room for error.

■ Always double check measurements before cutting your fabric.

■ If using a fabric that is printed off-grain, cut the pieces following the print, not the grain of the fabric.

■ Cut the longest border pieces first. This way you are less likely to run out of fabric.

■ For an interesting effect, use pieced fabric to create your border.

■ Cut sashing and border strips with a rotary cutter, rather than scissors, to achieve a perfectly straight edge.

Mitred corners

Cut side borders to measure the same length as the sides of the quilt top plus twice the border width plus 5cm (2"). Cut upper and lower borders to measure the same length as the ends of the quilt top plus twice the border width plus 5cm (2").

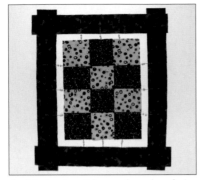

1. Mark the sides and ends of the quilt top with pins at the quarter and halfway points. Ensure the border strips are marked in the same manner (see page 82).

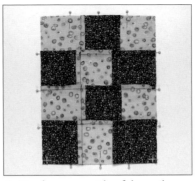

2. On the wrong side of the quilt top, mark the position at each corner where the stitchlines cross.

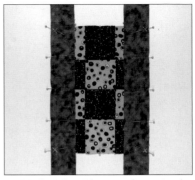

3. With right sides together, pin the side borders to the quilt top. Transfer the marked corner spots to the borders by pushing a pin through at each mark and marking the border where the pin emerges.

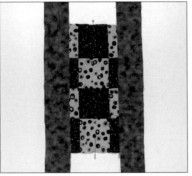

4. Starting and finishing at the marked spots, stitch the side borders in place.

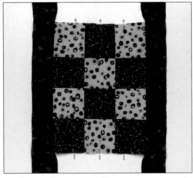

5. Press the seam allowances towards the borders.

6. Pin the upper and lower border pieces to the quilt top and mark the corner spots in the same manner as before.

SASHING AND BORDERS

■ If the border is made up of multiple strips of fabric, sew the strips together before making mitred corners.

■ Whether blocks are set horizontally or diagonally, always join the blocks, and any sashing, into rows and then join the rows together. If you are not using sashing, press the seams of alternate rows of blocks in opposite directions.

Mitred corners *continued*

7. Keeping the side borders out of the way and starting and finishing at the marked spots, stitch the upper and lower borders in place.

8. Press the seam allowances towards the borders.

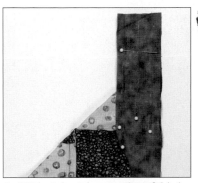

9. With right sides together, fold the quilt top in half diagonally. At one corner, temporarily fold the border seam allowances towards the quilt top and align the inner edges of the border pieces. Pin together.

10. On the wrong side, rule a line at a 45° angle from the end of the stitching to the opposite side of the border.

11. Starting exactly at the end of the previous stitching, stitch along the ruled line.

12. On the right side, ensure that the mitre will lay flat.

13. Trim the seam allowance to 6mm (1/4").

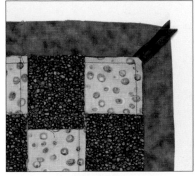

14. Press the seam open.

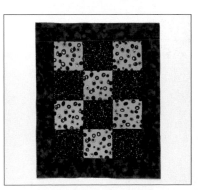

15. Form a mitre at the three remaining corners in the same manner.

Quilting

Quilts are like friends - a great source of comfort and warmth.

Anonymous

Marking the quilting design

There are several methods available to quilters for transferring the quilting design to the quilt top. Always test your chosen method on a scrap of fabric to ensure you can see the marks easily and to check that you can also remove them once the quilting is complete.

Before transferring the quilting design, carefully press the quilt top and trim any tails of thread. Trim away any points from seam allowances on the back of the fabric.

Stencils and templates

A large variety of stencils and templates can be purchased ready to use. You can also make your own, making them in the same manner as piecing templates (see pages 14 - 15). Ensure the quilt top is laid out on a firm, flat surface. Position the template or stencil on the right side of the quilt top and carefully trace around it or along the design lines using your selected marking tool.

1. Lightly trace around a template with a fine lead pencil. Use a mechanical pencil so the thickness of the lines remains consistent.

2. When using the pencil to transfer a stencil, keep the pencil as upright as possible.

3. Chalk markers can be used and are particularly useful for dark fabrics. You need to take care that the marks are not brushed away before the quilting is complete.

4. Special quilters coloured pencils can also be used. Ensure you sharpen them frequently so your lines stay as fine as possible.

5. Place the quilt top over a piece of flannel. Using a stiletto or blunt rug making needle and pressing firmly, trace the template or stencil. This method works best on natural fabrics.

6. On dark fabric, trace around the template or stencil with a sliver of soap. Frequently check the width of the marking edge as it will dull fairly quickly.

Perforated patterns

1. Trace the design onto paper.

2. Machine stitch along the design lines with a large unthreaded needle.

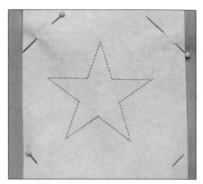

3. Position the pattern onto the right side of the quilt top.

4. Rub cornstarch, cinnamon or pounce (depending on the colour of the fabric) through the holes in the paper.

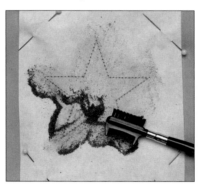

5. Brush away the excess.

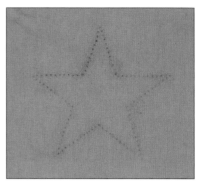

6. Remove the pattern. Dotted lines remain on the fabric.

Tracings - method one

This method of tracing is only suitable for light coloured and thin fabrics.

1. Trace the design onto paper with a black pen.

2. Place the tracing onto a light box or window. Position the quilt top over the tracing.

3. Trace over the design lines using your selected marking tool (see stencils and templates on page 87).

Tracings - method two

1. Cover the design with thin plastic. Place a piece of tulle over the design. Trace the design with a black pen.

2. Position the tulle on the quilt top and trace over the design lines using your selected marking tool (see stencils and templates on page 87).

3. Remove the tulle and dotted lines will mark the stitching lines.

Masking tape

This method is only suitable for marking straight lines and the tape should not be left on the fabric for extended periods as it may leave glue behind.

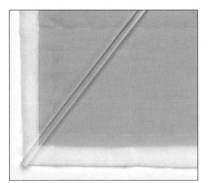

1. On the right side of the quilt top, place a ruler where you want to mark a quilting line.

2. Place the masking tape alongside the ruler.

3. Quilting will be done along the edge of the masking tape.

quilting marking the design

....

89

QUILTING DESIGNS

■ Ensure your quilting design will allow the density of the stitching to be relatively uniform over the entire quilt.

■ When using a lead pencil for marking designs use a HB lead.

These pencils keep their points longer and are easier to erase. Don't use a pencil with a lead softer than 2B.

■ Keep the distances between quilting lines in proportion to the scale of the quilting design.

Attaching the batting and lining Preparing the lining

1. Cut away selvedges and press. Cut out the lining to the size of the quilt top plus 10cm (4") longer and wider.

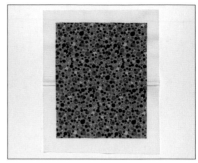

2. Alternatively, cut lengths of fabric and sew together. Press the seams open.

3. Cut out the lining to the measurements in step 1.

Layering

1. Spread the lining out flat, face down onto a large flat surface (eg floor or large table). Hold in place with masking tape. Mark the centre of each side.

2. Cut batting the same size as the lining. Fold into quarters. Position it onto one quarter of the lining. Align the edges and folds of the batting with the lining's edges and centre marks.

3. Gently unfold the batting, taking care not to stretch it. Carefully smooth out any wrinkles.

4. With the right side to the inside, fold the quilt top in quarters. Position it onto one quarter of the batting, aligning the folds with the centre marks. The raw edges should be an even 5cm (2") inside the batting.

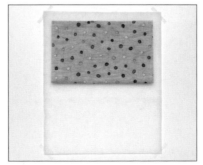

5. Gently unfold the quilt top to cover half of the batting. Smooth out with all cut edges 5cm (2") inside the batting.

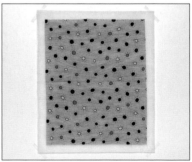

6. Unfold the remaining half. Carefully smooth it out, taking care not to stretch it or pull it out of shape.

If the quilt is to be self-bound, adjust the lining measurement to suit the width of the desired self binding.

Basting with safety pins

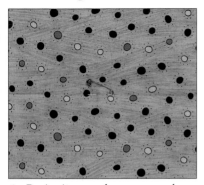

1. Beginning at the centre, take a safety pin through all three layers. Do not close the safety pin.

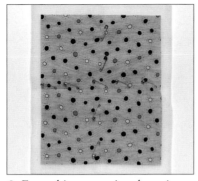

2. From this centre pin, place pins at regular intervals out to one side and end of the quilt along the centre lines. Place the pins approximately 8cm - 10cm (3" - 4") apart.

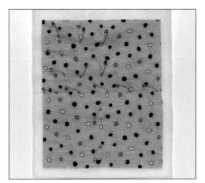

3. Smoothing the quilt top as you go, continue placing pins in one quarter of the quilt. Avoid pinning exactly on the marked quilting lines.

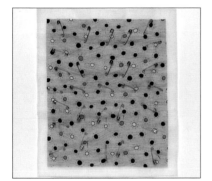

4. Pin the three remaining quarters in the same manner.

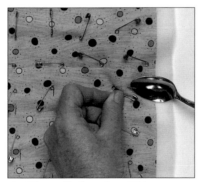

5. Close all the pins. Using a tea-spoon can make this easier. Slide the bowl under the tip of the pin and twist slightly to lift the tip and catch it.

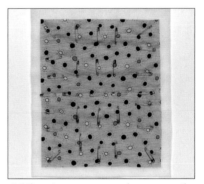

6. The pins are removed as you quilt.

HINTS ON BASTING

■ Store your safety pins, open, in a lidded box. This will save you considerable time on your next quilt. A full size quilt will require approximately 500 pins!

■ Keep pins sharp by inserting the tips into an emery strawberry. Push the pin into the strawberry, hold the strawberry firmly to compress the emery inside, then rotate the pin to sharpen it.

■ When basting with thread, use a light coloured thread that contrasts with your quilt. Dark coloured threads may permanently mark the quilt.

■ Make your basting stitches approximately 5cm (2") long on the top of the quilt and 12mm (1/2") long on the underside.

Basting with thread

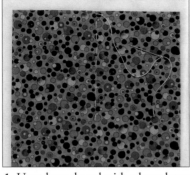

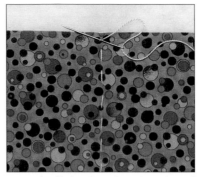

1. Use a long thread with a large knot in the end and a long needle (eg darning needle). Beginning at the centre, work long running stitches to the top of the quilt.

2. End off the thread at the edge of the quilt top with two small back stitches.

3. Again beginning from the centre, stitch to the lower edge and end off the thread in the same manner.

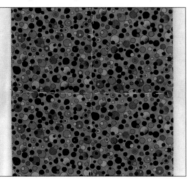

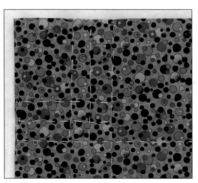

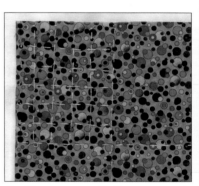

4. Repeat the procedure, stitching from the centre to one side of the quilt and then from the centre to the opposite side.

5. Starting near the centre basting each time, begin to fill in one quarter of the quilt with a grid of stitching lines approximately 8cm - 10cm (3" - 4") apart.

6. Continue until the quarter is completely covered.

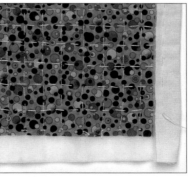

7. Work the remaining quarters in the same manner.

8. Fold the excess batting and lining on one edge onto the right side of the quilt top. Tack in place.

9. Continue around all sides to form a temporary binding. This will help prevent the edges from fraying as you quilt.

Quilting by hand Knotting the thread

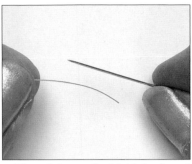

1. Thread the needle. Hold the thread against the tip of the needle approximately 2.5cm (1") from the end.

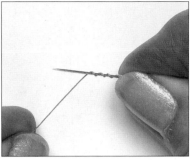

2. Wrap the thread around the tip of the needle three times.

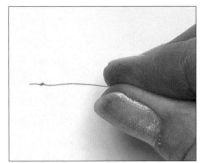

3. Hold the wraps firmly and begin to pull the needle through. Pull until a knot forms near the end of the thread.

This method creates a knot just the right size for quilting.

Starting the thread

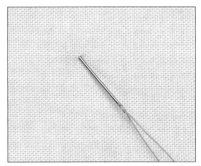

1. Beginning on the right side, insert the needle into the quilt top approximately 15mm (5/8") away from the starting point.

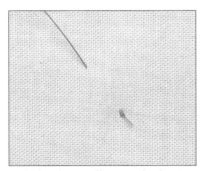

2. Take the needle into the batting and re-emerge at the starting position. Pull the thread through until the knot lies on the surface of the fabric.

3. Gently tug the thread to sink the knot beneath the surface.

Ending off the thread

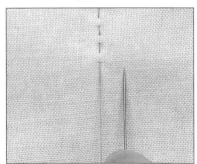

1. Pull the thread taut towards you. Hold the needle on the right hand side of the thread so it points towards the fabric.

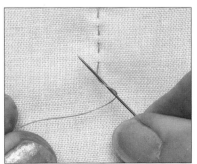

2. Take the needle over and then under the thread to form a wrap around the needle.

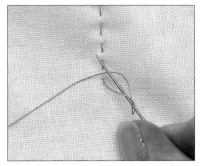

3. Pick up the thread and take it from right to left behind the tip of the needle. The thread around the needle will resemble a figure eight.

Ending off the thread *continued*

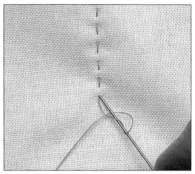

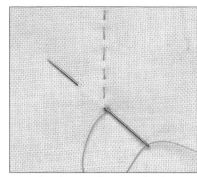

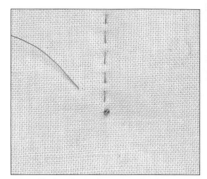

4. Place the tip of the needle into the fabric through exactly the same hole from which it last emerged.

5. Take the needle into the batting and re-emerge through the quilt top a short distance away.

6. Pull the thread taut so the knot lies on the surface.

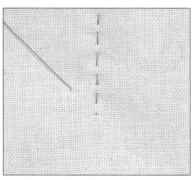

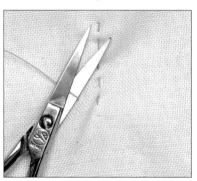

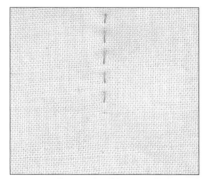

7. Give the thread a gentle tug to sink the knot beneath the surface.

8. Pull the thread firmly to slightly pucker the fabric. Cut the thread close to the fabric.

9. Smooth out the fabric and the tail will disappear beneath the surface

Quilting without a hoop or frame

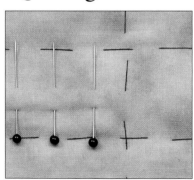

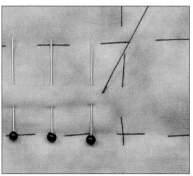

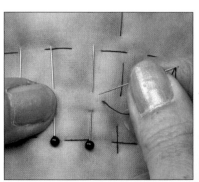

1. Place one hand below and one above the quilt and smooth the fabric along the line to be quilted. Pinning through all layers, place several pins across this line.

2. Secure the thread following the instructions on page 93.

3. Firmly hold a section of the quilt in one hand with fingers below and thumb on top. Hold the needle so it lies above your hand rather than below (a bit like holding a pen).

Quilting without a hoop or frame *continued*

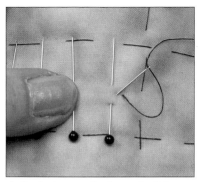

4. Push the needle through all layers until approximately half the needle extends from the back.

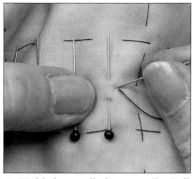

5. Hold the needle horizontally. Pull it backwards and run the tip along the lining fabric, with your fingers following, until it is at the spot you want to bring it to the front.

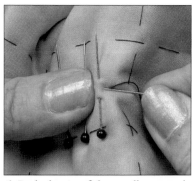

6. Push the tip of the needle upwards with your fingers, applying pressure from the top with your thumb, until the tip is as close as possible to 90° to the fabric.

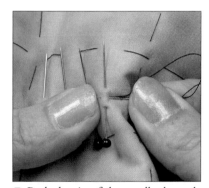

7. Push the tip of the needle through the quilt.

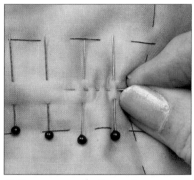

8. Repeat steps 4 - 7, putting as many stitches on the needle as you can comfortably manage.

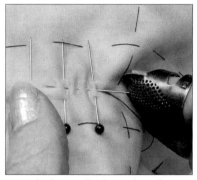

9. Push the needle through with your middle finger.

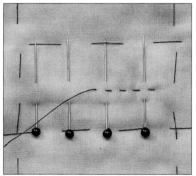

10. Pull the thread through.

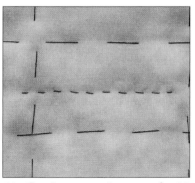

11. Continue repeating steps 4 - 10 for the entire line of quilting.

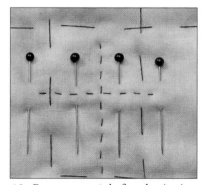

12. Repeat step 1 before beginning each new line of quilting unless other lines of quilting already stabilize the layers of fabric.

quilting quilting by hand

Quilting in a hoop or frame

While you don't always have a choice, it is best to quilt towards yourself wherever possible. Before you start, secure the thread following the instructions on page 93.

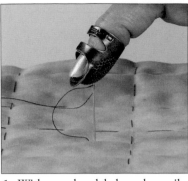

1. With one hand below the quilt, balance the needle at a 90° angle on the top of the quilt. Do not push it through.

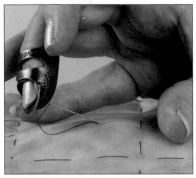

2. Gently guiding and rocking the needle with your middle finger only, push it through until you just feel the tip on the underside.

3. Lay the needle all the way back so the tip is pointing upwards. Push upwards with the finger below the quilt while pushing downwards with your thumb at the position immediately in front of the tip of the needle.

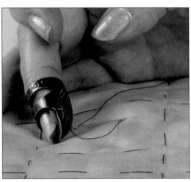

4. Re-apply pressure to the end of the needle with your middle finger to force it back up to the surface. Stop pushing as soon as the tip of the needle is visible.

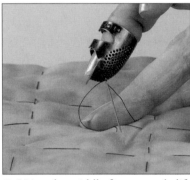

5. Using the middle finger, gently lift the needle until it is at a 90° angle to the top of the quilt and you can barely feel the tip on the underside.

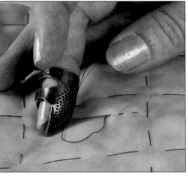

6. Repeat steps 1 - 5 to place a second stitch on the needle.

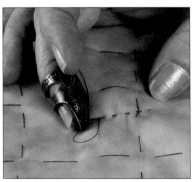

7. Continue repeating steps 1 - 5 until you cannot return the needle to a 90° angle to the top of the quilt.

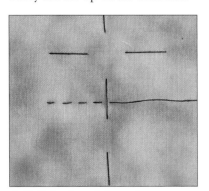

8. Pull the thread through.

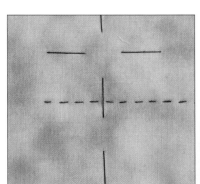

9. Continue repeating steps 1 - 8 for the entire line of quilting.

quilting quilting by hand

············

96

Quilting by machine
Starting and finishing

The threads need to be locked in position at the beginning and end of each line of stitching. This prevents them unravelling at a later date and also ensures that your stitching starts and ends exactly where you want it to.

method one

1. Place the quilt under the presser foot and lower the needle into the fabric at the position you wish to start stitching.

2. Set the stitch length to 0. Work several stitches, finishing with the needle in the down position.

3. Adjust the stitch length to the desired length of your quilting stitch and continue stitching.

4. Repeat step 2 to secure the thread at the end of the line.

5. Trim the tails of thread to approximately 2.5cm (1").

method two

1. Place the quilt under the presser foot and lower the needle into the fabric at the position you wish to start stitching.

2. Use the securing function built into your sewing machine (if available).

3. Continue stitching.

4. Repeat step 2 to secure the thread at the end of the line.

5. Trim the tails of thread to approximately 2.5cm (1").

method three

1. Place the quilt under the presser foot and lower the needle into the fabric at the position you wish to start stitching.

2. Set the stitch length to the desired length for your quilting stitch. As you begin to stitch, hold the fabric firmly so it cannot move for the first few stitches.

3. Release the pressure on the fabric and continue stitching.

4. Repeat step 2 to secure the thread at the end of the line.

5. Trim the tails of thread to approximately 2.5cm (1").

method four

1. Place the quilt under the presser foot and lower the needle into the fabric at the position you wish to start stitching.

2. Set the stitch length to the desired length for your quilting stitch. Work forward for approximately three stitches.

3. Stitch in reverse back to the beginning and then stitch forward.

4. Reverse the procedure to secure the thread at the end of the line.

5. Trim the tails of thread to approximately 2.5cm (1").

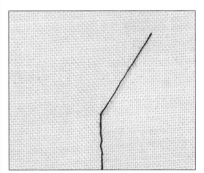

method one

method three

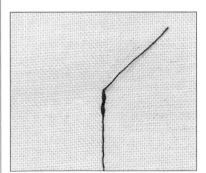

method two

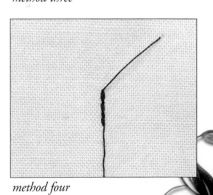

method four

Trimming the tails of thread

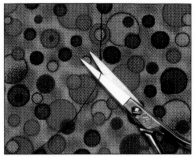

1. Cut the thread on the top of the quilt as close as possible to the fabric.

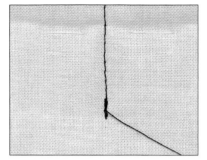

2. Turn the quilt over. Give the bobbin thread a gentle tug to pull the end of the top thread into the batting.

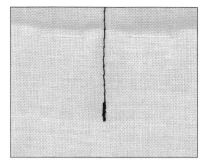

3. Cut the bobbin thread as close as possible to the fabric.

Quilting with the feed dog engaged

1. Engage the walking foot on your machine and set the stitch length to 2.5. Lock the threads at the beginning of the stitchline using your chosen method (see page 97).

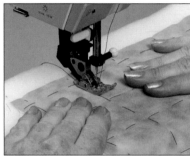

2. As you stitch, hold the fabric on either side, and just in front of the presser foot with both hands to keep it smooth.

3. To work near the centre of the quilt, feed the quilt from left to right under the raised presser foot. Roll up the section of quilt on the right as you feed it through.

Free motion quilting

Spend time practicing and experimenting to discover the machine speed and quilt movement that is most comfortable for you.

1. Disengage the feed dog. Attach a darning foot or special quilting foot. Lock the threads using your chosen method (see page 97).

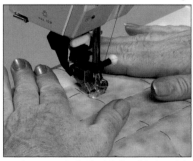

2. As you stitch, hold the fabric with both hands held flat and encircling the needle.

3. Maintaining a steady speed, smoothly move the quilt in the desired directions with your hands.

QUILTING BY MACHINE

■ Always use a new needle for each new quilting project.

■ If possible, have the surface of your sewing machine's feed dog level with the surrounding table. This will help reduce drag and the quilt will feed through more evenly.

■ Place a second table to the left of your chair, butting it up against the sewing machine table to form an L-shape. This will help support the quilt as you stitch.

■ Ensure the walking foot of your sewing machine is attached or engaged. This will help keep the layers together as they move below the needle.

■ Whenever you stop stitching, always ensure the needle is in the down position.

■ Quilt the longest lines first and then fill in with the shorter lines of stitching.

■ Ensure that the section of the quilt in front of and to the sides of the needle is always smooth and flat.

■ If your hands do not seem to be holding the quilt firmly enough, wear cotton gloves with rubber tips on the fingers for added grip.

■ Always work a test sample to check stitch length and tension before stitching on your quilt.

Straight line quilting

Plan the route your quilting will take to minimise the number of times you need to end off the thread.

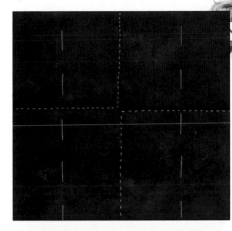

Quilting in the ditch

Stitch in the seamlines around and within the pieced blocks. This is an excellent way to stabilize your quilt.
If using this method, it should be completed before continuing with any other quilting.

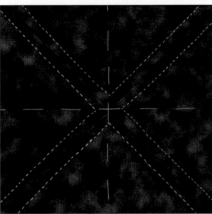

Outline quilting

Stitch alongside the seamlines around and within the blocks. Take care to keep the stitching the same distance from the seamlines at all times.

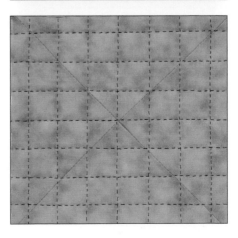

Grid or cross-hatch quilting

Working backwards and forwards across the fabric, stitch all the lines in one direction, keeping them evenly spaced. When these are complete, stitch all lines at 90° to the first set of lines.

Echo quilting

1. Quilt around the edge of the appliquéd shape, finishing where you began stitching.

2. Work a second row of quilting, keeping the stitching an equal distance from the shape on all sides. Again, finish where you began.

3. Work a third row in the same manner, keeping it an equal distance from the second line of stitching at all times.

4. If machine quilting, lock the thread at the beginning and end off each row but do cut. Move to the next row, carrying the thread each time.

5. Continue working rows in the same manner, ensuring they are evenly spaced.

6. Trim away the carried threads on both the front and back of the machine quilted quilt.

Corded quilting

1. Cut a piece of fabric for the top and mark the design on the right side. Using a loose weave fabric (eg muslin), cut the backing piece the same size.

2. Place the two fabrics wrong sides together and baste.

3. Hand or machine quilt along the design lines, forming channels.

Corded quilting *continued*

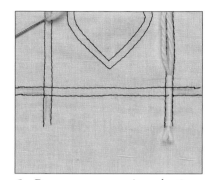

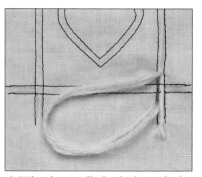

4. Thread a large, blunt needle with wool. With the wrong side uppermost, take the needle into the beginning of a channel through the backing fabric only.

5. Re-emerge approximately 3cm (1 1/8") away. Pull the yarn through leaving a short tail extending at the beginning.

6. Take the needle back through the same hole in the backing fabric and slide it along the channel.

7. Re-emerge approximately 3cm (1 1/8") away. Leaving a small loop on the back of the fabric, pull the yarn through.

8. Continue in this manner until the channel is filled. Cut off the excess yarn, leaving a short tail extending. If two channels cross, cut the yarn at this point so it doesn't overlap another section of yarn.

9. Fill all channels in the same manner.

10. Using the end of a blunt needle, push the ends and loops of yarn into the channels.

11. With the right side uppermost, place the quilted fabric over the batting and lining. Baste in place (see pages 91 - 92).

12. Quilt along each channel, just outside the previous stitching.

Trapunto - method one

1. Cut two pieces of fabric, one for the top and one for the backing. Mark the design on the right side of the top fabric. Ensure the design includes shapes that will be completely surrounded by stitching.

2. Place the two fabrics wrong sides together and baste.

3. Hand or machine quilt around the design.

4. Using small, sharp-ended scissors and cutting along the grain through the backing fabric only, cut a small opening inside one shape.

5. Push filling through the opening, pushing it right to the edges of the stitching and into any corners.

6. Overcast the edges of the opening together.

7. Repeat steps 4 - 6 in all the desired shapes.

8. With the right side uppermost, place the quilted fabric over the batting and lining. Baste in place (see pages 91 - 92).

9. Quilt along each filled shape, just outside the previous stitching. Remove the basting.

method two

1. Mark the design on the right side of the top fabric. Ensure the design includes shapes that will be completely surrounded by stitching.

2. Cut a piece of thick batting and a piece of lining, both approximately 2.5cm (1") larger than the design.

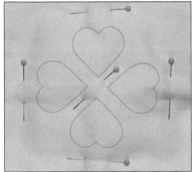

3. Place the batting over the lining and position them behind the design on the quilt top. Pin in place from the front.

4. Using water-soluble basting thread in the needle and normal sewing thread in the bobbin, machine stitch along the design lines.

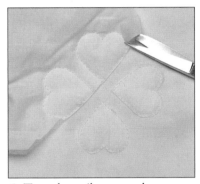

5. Turn the quilt over and cut away the excess batting and lining as close as possible to the stitching.

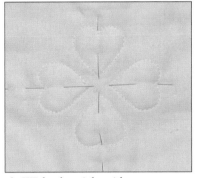

6. With the right side uppermost, place the quilted fabric over the batting and lining. Baste in place (see pages 91 - 92).

7. Machine stitch around the design, stitching directly on top of the previous stitching.

8. Work the desired quilting on the remainder of the quilt.

9. Spray the quilt top with water to dissolve the water-soluble basting thread.

Tying Buttoning

These two tying techniques work particularly well on quilts that use very thick or puffy batting.

1. Add extra pins to ensure that the area around the button position is flat. Knot a doubled thread and take it from the front into the batting. Re-emerge at the position for the button.

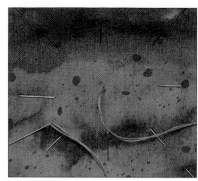

2. Sink the knot into the quilt.

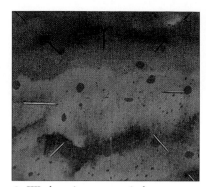

3. Work a tiny cross stitch to secure the thread.

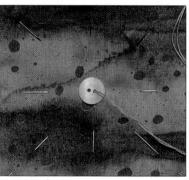

4. Position the button on the fabric. Take the needle up through the quilt and button.

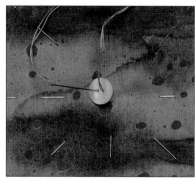

5. Take the needle down through the button and all layers of the quilt.

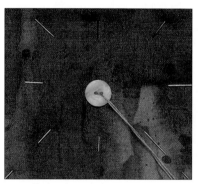

6. Pull the thread through. Bring the needle back up through all layers, including the button.

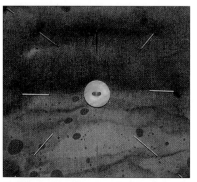

7. Work several more stitches through all layers. Pull the thread firmly but not too tight.

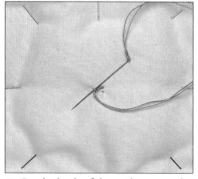

8. On the back of the quilt, secure the thread with two tiny back stitches.

9. Take the thread into the batting and re-emerge. Pull the thread and cut close to the fabric. The tail will disappear inside the quilt.

Tufting

1. Add extra pins to ensure that the area around the tufting position is flat.

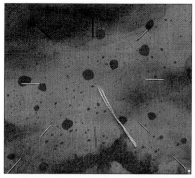

2. Using a doubled thread, take it from the front to the back, leaving a 3cm (1 1/8") tail of thread on the front.

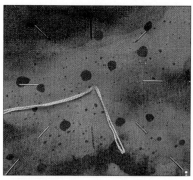

3. Bring the thread to the front close to where it first went through the quilt.

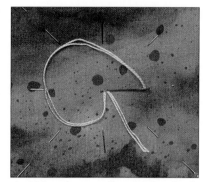

4. Take the needle to the back through the first hole.

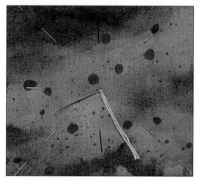

5. Pull the thread through. Bring the thread to the front through the second hole.

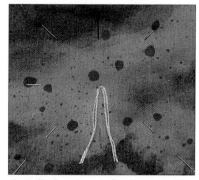

6. Pull the thread firmly. Trim the thread to the same length as the first tail.

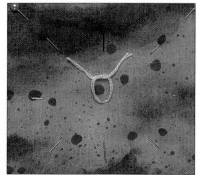

7. Holding one tail in each hand, wrap the left tail over and under the right tail.

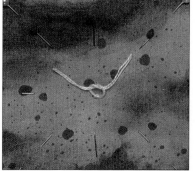

8. Pull tightly, then wrap the new right tail over and under the new left tail.

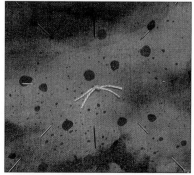

9. Pull tightly. Trim the tails to the required length.

Finishing

Our lives are like quilts - bits and pieces

joy and sorrow, stitched with love.

Anonymous

Squaring the quilt Blocking

1. Fold the excess batting and lining over the quilt top and hand baste in place.

2. Hand or machine wash the quilt. Lay the damp quilt on a carpeted floor covered with sheets (or similar flat surface). Remove the basting and smooth out the quilt.

3. Using a metal tape measure, measure the length of the quilt through the centre and along each side. Stretch or ease the sides to match the centre measurement.

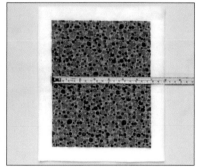

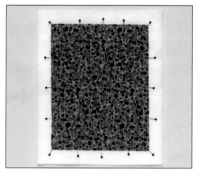

4. Repeat step 3 across the width of the quilt.

5. Measure diagonally across the quilt from corner to corner. Tug on the corners until the measurement is identical across both diagonals.

6. Smooth the corners so they look square. Leave the quilt to dry. If required, pin the edge of the quilt to the floor to ensure it remains in place.

Squaring

1. Using a large square ruler and using the outermost border seam as an additional guide, line up two adjacent sides of the quilt. Rule lines to mark the straight edges of the quilt.

2. Change to a long straight ruler and continue marking in the same manner along the sides. Continue in the same manner around the entire quilt top.

3. Engage the walking foot and stitch a row of machine basting along the marked line. Ensure the needle is down each time you pivot. The quilt is now ready for binding.

Binding Joining bias strips

Binding strips can be cut on the bias or on the straight grain of the fabric. However, binding strips cut on the straight grain are more likely to ripple and buckle. If the binding is to be curved, bias cut strips are a must.

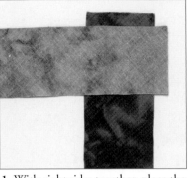

1. With right sides together, place the ends of two strips at right angles. Allow the ends of the strips to extend beyond each other by approx 6mm ($1/4$").

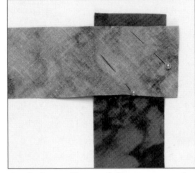

2. Rule a diagonal line across the upper strip from corner to corner. Pin the strips together.

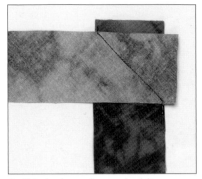

3. Stitch along the marked line.

4. Leaving a 6mm ($1/4$") seam allowance, trim away the excess fabric.

5. Press the seam open.

6. Cut off the small triangles of seam allowance that extend beyond the sides of the strip.

Making continuous bias binding

1. Cut a large square of fabric. Fold it diagonally in half and press the fold.

2. Unfold and cut the fabric along the foldline.

3. With right sides together, place the two triangles so the edges meet along one short side of each triangle and the long sides are at right angles. Pin.

Making continuous bias binding *continued*

4. Stitch using a 6mm (¹/₄") seam allowance. Press the seam open.

5. Decide on the width of bias strip you require. Rule lines across the fabric parallel to one bias edge, keeping them evenly spaced and at the required measurement.

6. With right sides together, fold the fabric so the diagonal ends meet. Offset the ends so the first line on one edge is aligned with the edge of the fabric.

7. Pin the ends, right sides together, ensuring the lines match at the stitchline.

8. Stitch using a 6mm (¹/₄") seam allowance.

9. Press the seam open.

10. Turn to the right side.

11. Cut along the marked line with scissors.

12. Alternatively place a cutting mat on the ironing board. Using a rotary cutter, cut along the marked lines, moving the tube around the ironing board, as you need.

Attaching doubled binding with butted corners

1. Cut the binding strips four times the desired finished width plus 2.5cm (1"). With wrong sides together, fold the strips in half along the length and press.

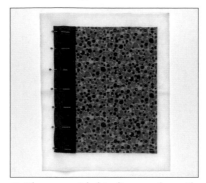

2. Place one side binding on the quilt so the raw edges of the binding are aligned with the raw edge of the quilt top. Pin in place.

3. Stitch in place using a 6mm (¼") seam allowance.

4. Measure out the finished width of the binding from the seamline. Trim away the excess batting and lining fabric beyond this measurement.

5. Press the binding away from the quilt top.

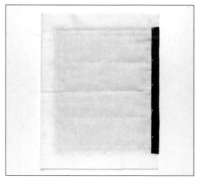

6. Fold the binding to the back. Pin in place so the folded edge of the binding just covers the stitchline.

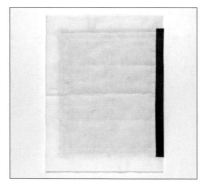

7. Using thread to match the binding, hand stitch the binding to the lining. Do not take the stitches through to the front of the quilt.

8. Attach the binding to the opposite side in the same manner.

9. Cut the upper binding strip 5cm (2") longer than the width of the quilt top plus side binding pieces. Mark the strip 2.5cm (1") in from each end.

Attaching doubled binding with butted corners *continued*

10. Match raw edges and align the marks with the finished sides of the quilt. Pin and stitch the strip to the right side of the quilt, stitching across the ends of the binding as well.

11. Trim the ends of the binding to 1cm (³/8") beyond the stitching. Trim away the excess batting and lining as before.

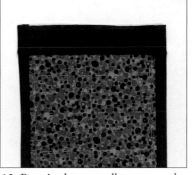

12. Press in the seam allowance at the ends along the stitchlines.

13. Press the binding away from the quilt top as before.

14. Fold the binding to the back. Pin in place so the folded edge of the binding just covers the stitchline.

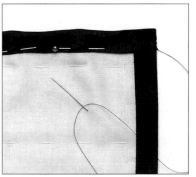

15. Hand stitch the folded ends of the binding together at one end.

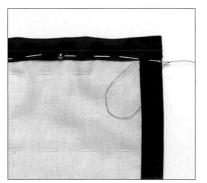

16. Hand stitch the top binding to the side binding.

17. Continue stitching the binding to the lining and the remaining folded end. Do not take the stitches through to the front of the quilt.

18. Attach the binding to the opposite end in the same manner.

finishing binding

....

111

Attaching single binding with butted corners

1. Cut the binding strips twice the desired finished width plus 12mm (¹/2"). Lightly press under 6mm (¹/4") along one long side of each strip.

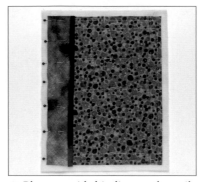

2. Place one side binding on the quilt so the unfolded raw edge of the binding is aligned with the raw edge of the quilt top. Pin in place.

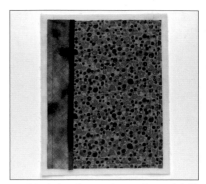

3. Stitch in place using a 6mm (¹/4") seam allowance.

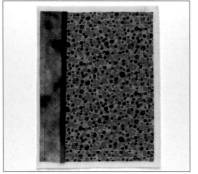

4. Measure out the finished width of the binding from the seamline. Trim away the excess batting and lining fabric beyond this measurement.

5. Press the binding away from the quilt top.

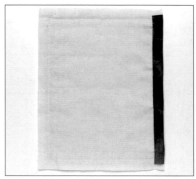

6. Fold the binding to the back. Pin in place so the folded edge of the binding just covers the stitchline.

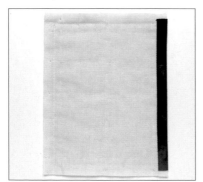

7. Using thread to match the binding, hand stitch the binding to the lining. Do not take the stitches through to the front of the quilt.

8. Attach the binding to the opposite side in the same manner.

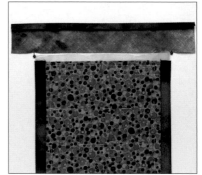

9. Cut the upper binding strip 5cm (2") longer than the width of the quilt top plus side binding pieces. Mark the strip 2.5cm (1") in from each end.

Attaching single binding with butted corners *continued*

10. Matching raw edges and aligning the marks with the finished sides of the quilt, pin the strip to the right side of the quilt.

11. Stitch in place, stitching across the ends of the binding as well.

12. Trim the ends of the binding to 1cm (³/₈") beyond the stitching. Trim away the excess batting and lining as before.

13. Press in the seam allowance at the ends along the stitchlines.

14. Press the binding away from the quilt top as before.

15. Fold the binding to the back. Pin in place so the folded edge of the binding just covers the stitchline.

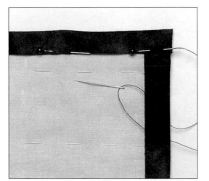

16. Hand stitch the folded ends of the binding together at one end.

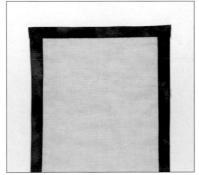

17. Continue stitching the binding to the lining and the remaining folded end. Do not take the stitches through to the front of the quilt.

18. Attach the binding to the opposite end in the same manner.

Attaching doubled binding with mitred corners

Cut the binding strips four times the desired finished width plus 2.5cm (1").

1. Join the strips to make one continuous length. With wrong sides together, fold the strip in half along the length and press.

2. Beginning near the middle on one side, pin the binding to the first corner of the quilt. Keep the raw edges of the binding and quilt top aligned.

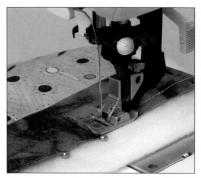

3. Leaving the first 15cm (6") of pinned binding unstitched, begin stitching towards the corner using a 6mm (1/4") seam allowance.

4. When approx 5cm (2") from the corner, stop with the needle down. Raise the presser foot, turn back the binding edge and mark the quilt top 6mm (1/4") in from its edges.

5. Place a pin at the marked spot. Continue stitching until reaching the pin. End off the thread.

6. Remove the quilt from the machine and turn it so the stitching is at the top.

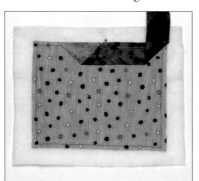

7. Fold the binding strip up at a 45° angle. Press.

8. Fold the strip down along the adjacent side of the quilt top, aligning raw edges as before. Hold the fold in place with a pin. Pin the strip to the quilt in the same manner as before.

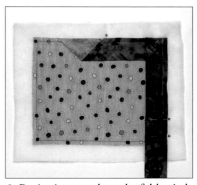

9. Beginning exactly at the fold, stitch until approximately 5cm (2") from the next corner.

Attaching doubled binding with mitred corners *continued*

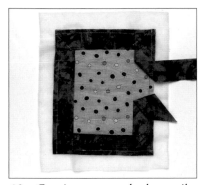

10. Continue around the quilt, forming the corners and stitching until approximately 20cm (8") from where you first started stitching.

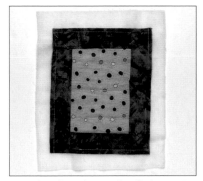

11. Turn under a 6mm (¹/₄") seam allowance at the beginning of the binding strip and press.

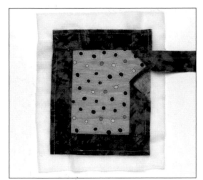

12. Overlay the end of the strip. Leaving a 2cm (³/₄") overlap, trim away any excess binding.

13. Pin and stitch the remaining section of binding in place.

14. Measure out the finished width of the binding from the seamline. Trim away the excess batting and lining fabric beyond this measurement.

15. Press the binding away from the quilt top.

16. Fold the binding to the back and press again. Pin the binding in place. Pin the mitres on the back of the quilt.

17. Using thread to match the binding, hand stitch the binding to the lining. Do not take the stitches through to the front of the quilt.

18. Hand stitch the mitres in place.

Attaching single binding with mitred corners

1. Trim the binding to twice the desired finished width plus 12mm (¹/₂"). Press under 6mm (¹/₄") along one long side.

2. Beginning near the middle on one side, place the binding on the quilt so the unfolded raw edge of the binding is aligned with the raw edge of the quilt top. Pin the binding in place to the first corner.

3. Attach the binding in the same manner as the doubled binding with mitred corners.

Rounded corners

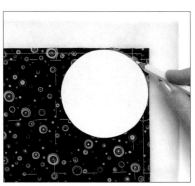

1. Trace the shape of the curve onto each corner (a plate makes a good template for this).

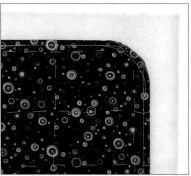

2. Baste around the corners, overlapping the previous basting along the sides. Trim the quilt top along the marked curves.

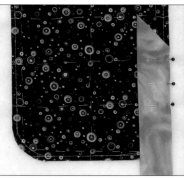

3. Starting along one side and using a doubled binding cut on the bias, pin the binding to the quilt top so the raw edges are aligned.

HINTS ON BINDING

■ Before sewing binding in place, lay it around the quilt to ensure that no joins in the binding will fall at the corners.

■ If your sewing machine has a walking foot, use it when attaching binding. It will make it easier to ensure all layers of fabric are fed through the machine at the same rate.

■ To make a long length of binding easier to manage, roll it onto a cylinder or spool. Take care not to stretch the binding.

■ As you sew, keep your binding in your lap. If it hangs over your sewing table it may become stretched by its own weight.

■ A doubled binding is a good choice for bed quilts as it is less likely to wear as quickly as a single binding.

Rounded corners *continued*

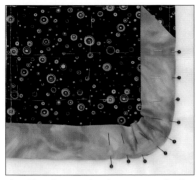

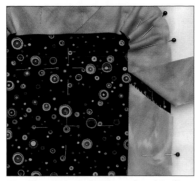

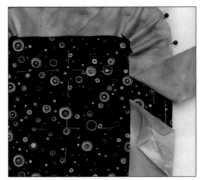

4. Continue pinning around the corner, taking care not to stretch the binding and keeping the raw edges aligned.

5. Continue pinning the binding around the entire quilt in the same manner until approx 20cm (8") from where you first started pinning.

6. Turn under a 6mm (¹/₄") seam allowance at the beginning of the binding strip and press.

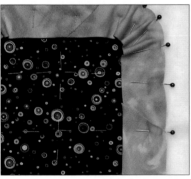

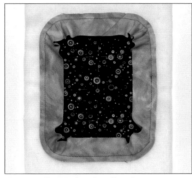

7. Overlay the end of the strip. Leaving a 2cm (³/₄") overlap, trim away any excess binding.

8. Stitch with the binding uppermost, carefully easing any tucks that form around the curves.

9. Measure out the finished width of the binding from the seamline. Trim away the excess batting and lining fabric beyond this measurement.

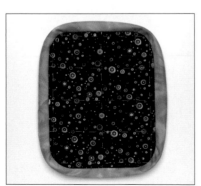

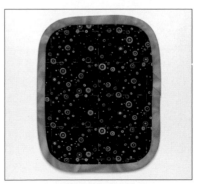

10. Fold the binding to the back. Press with the front uppermost, easing the edge of the binding so it lies flat.

11. Pin the binding in place on the back.

12. Using thread to match the binding, hand stitch the binding to the lining. Do not take the stitches through to the front of the quilt. Press.

Scallops

*Always use
fabric cut on
the bias when
binding
scallops.*

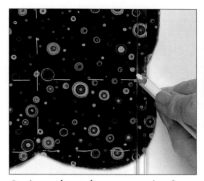

1. Mark the scallops on the quilt top. Baste 3mm ($1/8$") inside the marked lines.

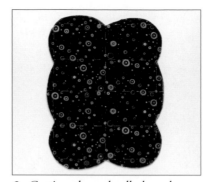

2. Cutting through all three layers, cut along the marked lines to remove the excess fabrics.

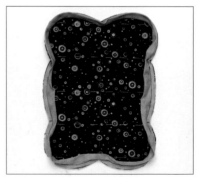

3. At each peak, measure in 6mm ($1/4$") from the edge and mark with a dot.

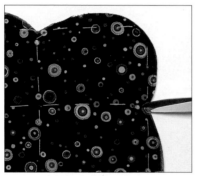

4. Using small, sharp scissors, clip from the outer edge of the peak towards the marked dots. Do not cut the dots.

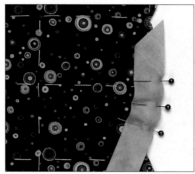

5. Beginning in the middle of a curve and aligning raw edges, begin to pin doubled binding to the front. Take care not to stretch the binding.

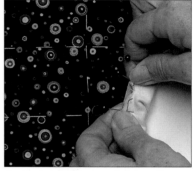

6. At the peak, spread the scallop to form a straight line. Pin the binding across the peak, ensuring the outer corners of the clipped peak align with the binding edge.

7. Continue around the entire quilt in the same manner.

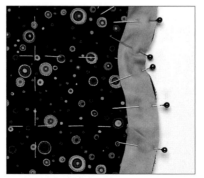

8. Turn under a 6mm ($1/4$") seam allowance at the beginning of the binding strip and press. Place the end of the strip over the beginning. Leaving a 2cm ($3/4$") overlap, trim away any excess binding.

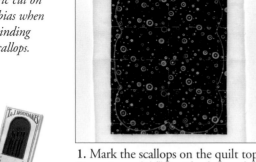

9. With the backing uppermost and using a 6mm ($1/4$") seam allowance, stitch around the entire quilt. Take care not to stretch the scallops.

Scallops *continued*

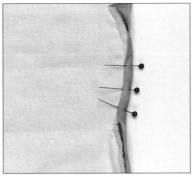

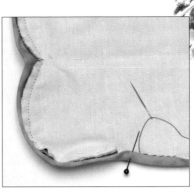

10. Gently press the binding away from the quilt.

11. Beginning in the middle of a scallop, fold the binding to the back. Pin the binding so the folded edge meets the stitchline, pinning almost to the adjacent peak.

12. Hand stitch the binding in place, finishing approximately 2.5cm (1") from the peak.

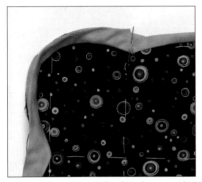

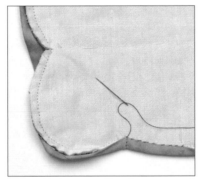

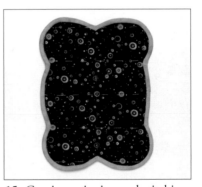

13. Fold and pin the binding at the peak.

14. Fold the mitred binding over and align the fold with the point of the peak. Pin and hand stitch in place, taking several stitches through the mitre.

15. Continue pinning and stitching, one scallop at a time, around the entire quilt. Press.

CURVED BINDING

■ To prevent puckers and creases, always use bias cut binding around curves.

■ To determine the length of binding you need for a scalloped edge, lay a piece of string or cord around the quilt, following the curves. When you have gone around the entire quilt, measure the piece of string or cord.

■ Narrow bindings (less than 15mm or 5/8") are less likely to pucker around curves than wide bindings.

■ Steam press the binding to encourage it to fit the shape of the curves.

■ Ensure the binding lies flat around the curves before stitching. If it cups slightly, remove the pins and adjust, taking care not to stretch the binding.

Backing turned to front

1. Using thread to match the lining, baste around the entire quilt 6mm (1/4") in from the edge of the quilt top.

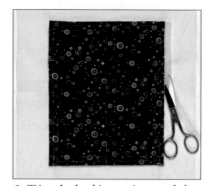

2. Trim the backing so it extends beyond the quilt top by twice the desired finished width. Trim the batting even with the edges of the quilt top.

3. With wrong sides together, fold over 6mm (1/4") along each side of the backing for the seam allowance. Press.

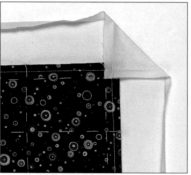

4. Unfold the seam allowances at one corner. Diagonally fold over the corner so the pressed foldlines lie along the basting. Finger press the fold.

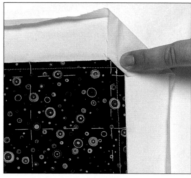

5. Fold back the tip of the triangle so you can see the basting at the corner and finger press.

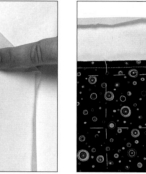

6. Cut along this second fold to remove the tip of the triangle. Secure the binding with a pin from the corner of the quilt top to the corner of the basting.

7. Repeat the procedure at each corner. Refold the seam allowance on one side.

8. Fold again so the folded edge is aligned with the basting. Pin in place. Fold and pin the three remaining sides in the same manner.

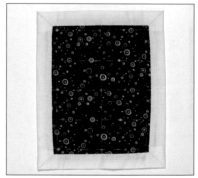

9. Using thread to match the binding, hand stitch the binding to the quilt top. Do not take the stitches through to the back of the quilt. Stitch the folds of the mitres together.

Adding a hanging sleeve

1. Cut a strip of fabric on the straight grain 22.5cm (9") wide and 2.5cm (1") shorter than the width of the quilt.

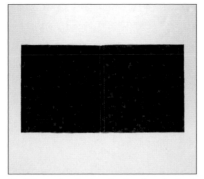

2. If required, to obtain the desired length, join pieces together and press the seams open. Stitch the edges of the seam allowances down.

3. With wrong sides together, fold under a double hem at each end and stitch in place. Press.

4. With wrong sides together, fold the strip in half along the length.

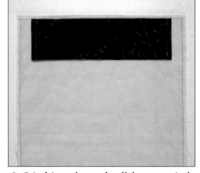

5. On the wrong side of the quilt, position the raw edges of the strip along the basting at the top of the quilt. Pin in place

6. Stitching through all layers, stitch the sleeve to the quilt just inside the seam allowance.

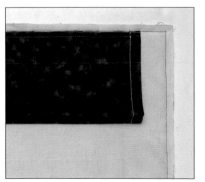

7. At the lower folded edge of the sleeve, make a small pleat. Press.

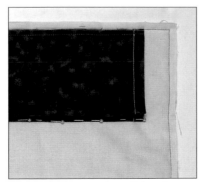

8. Pin the lower edge of the pleat to the quilt.

9. Hand stitch the lower edge of the ends and the pleat to the lining, ensuring the stitches do not go through to the front of the quilt.

If your quilt is to be displayed vertically, add a hanging sleeve before attaching the binding.

Glossary
Quilting terms

Appliqué - the application of smaller fabric shapes to a foundation fabric.

Backing - the fabric on the underside of a quilt, also known as lining.

Basting - temporarily holding fabrics together with stitches or safety pins.

Batting - the filling or middle layer of a quilt. It provides the bulk and warmth. Also known as wadding.

Bearding - when tiny fibres of batting poke through the quilt top or lining.

Bias - diagonal grain of fabric. The true bias is at exactly 45° to both the lengthwise and crosswise grains.

Block - the basic design unit that is repeated over the surface of a pieced quilt top.

Blocking - the process of re-shaping and sizing blocks or quilt tops so they are smooth and straight. Steam, heat, misted water or pressure are commonly used in blocking.

Border - fabric frame around the edge of the quilt top.

Cornerstones - the squares that connect sections of sashing or borders where they meet at the corners of blocks.

Fat quarter - piece of fabric measuring approximately 50cm x 57cm (18" x 22"), a half yard length of fabric cut in half down the length.

Foundation - background fabric used in appliqué, crazy patchwork and foundation piecing.

Fuse - to apply heat to a material with a heat activated glue so it glues to a piece of fabric.

Grain - the direction of the woven threads in a piece of fabric. The lengthwise grain runs parallel to the selvedges and the crosswise grain runs from selvedge to selvedge.

Hue - another word for colour.

Intensity - the pureness or brightness of a colour. Intensity is altered by adding or subtracting grey.

Lap quilting - quilting by hand without a hoop or frame.

Lining - the fabric on the underside of a quilt, also known as backing.

Loft - the thickness and resilience of batting.

Mitre - the corner join of a binding or border that creates a seam at a 45° angle.

Palette - the array of fabrics that are used within a quilt with particular emphasis on the range of colour.

Piecing - the technique of joining patches of fabric together to create a block.

Quilt top - the uppermost layer of a quilt.

Quilting - the process of securing the three layers of a quilt together.

Sandwich - the three layers of a quilt placed together. The first layer is the lining or backing, the second layer is the batting and the third layer is the quilt top.

Sashing - strips of fabric that are stitched between blocks.

Scale - the relative size of one object to another.

Seam allowance - the distance from a seam to the edge of the fabric. In patchwork and piecing this is always 6mm (1/4").

Selvedge - the woven band along each side of a length of fabric.

Shade - a hue created by adding black to the base colour.

Sleeve - a tube made from fabric which is attached to the back of the quilt. A rod is inserted through the tube so the quilt can be hung on a wall.

Stencil - card or plastic with a pattern or shape cut within it, that can be traced around to transfer a design onto fabric.

Template - a pattern or shape that can be traced around to transfer a design onto fabric, usually made from paper, card or plastic.

Tint - a hue created by adding white to the base colour.

Value - the lightness or darkness of a colour.

Wadding - the filling or middle layer of a quilt. It provides the bulk and warmth. Also known as batting.

Index

index

....

125

OTHER NEEDLEWORK TITLES AVAILABLE
FROM QUILTERS' RESOURCE

Needlework Books

Filled with beautiful projects,
easy instructions,
superb photography and
full size patterns.

Inspirations Baby

Inspirations Bridal

Inspirations Gifts

The World's Most Beautiful
Embroidered Blankets

Embroidered Christening Gowns

Embroidered Bags & Purses

The Embroiderer's Handbook

The Embroidered Village Bag

Quarterly Magazines

Each magazine features
stunning projects, magnificent
photography, clear step-by-step
instructions and full size
patterns.

Inspirations

Australian Smocking & Embroidery

THE A-Z SERIES

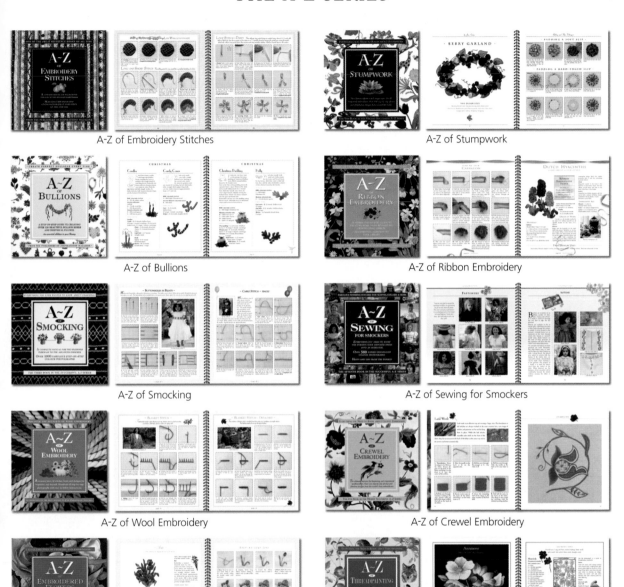

A-Z of Embroidery Stitches

A-Z of Stumpwork

A-Z of Bullions

A-Z of Ribbon Embroidery

A-Z of Smocking

A-Z of Sewing for Smockers

A-Z of Wool Embroidery

A-Z of Crewel Embroidery

A-Z of Embroidered Flowers

A-Z of Threadpainting *Coming soon*

Over 2,000,000 copies from the A-Z series have been sold worldwide. They are the ultimate reference books for needleworkers.

quilters' resource publications

. . . .

127

If you would like more information on any of these titles, please contact Quilters' Resource Inc.
PO Box 148850 Chicago, IL 60614 Phone: 773-278-5695

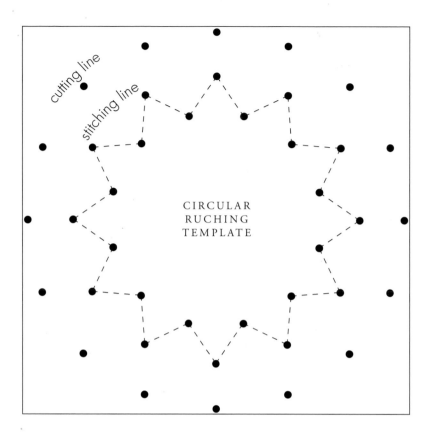

cutting line

stitching line

CIRCULAR
RUCHING
TEMPLATE

A very special thank you to Lizzie Kulinski, Marian Carpenter, Kathleen Barac, Sharon Venhoek, Heidi Reid, Anna Scott and Helen Davies for the hundreds of hours they spent in preparing photographic samples. Their talent and devotion has been both enriching and heartwarming.